Twayne's United States Authors Series

EDITOR OF THIS VOLUME

Kenneth Eble

University of Utah

Stanley Kunitz

TUSAS 351

STANLEY KUNITZ

By MARIE HÉNAULT

Saint Michael's College

TWAYNE PUBLISHERS
A DIVISION OF G. K. HALL & CO., BOSTON

811
K96zh

Library of Congress Cataloging in Publication Data
Hénault, Marie.
Stanley Kunitz.

(Twayne's United States authors series; TUSAS 351)
Bibliography: p. 154–59
Includes index.
1. Kunitz, Stanley Jasspon, 1905–
—Criticism and interpretation.
PS3521.U7Z69   811'.5'2   79–21086
ISBN 0-8057-7224-3

For
Robert J. Hénault
In Memoriam
1927–1978

Contents

About the Author

Marie Hénault is a professor of English at Saint Michael's College, Winooski, Vermont, where she teaches undergraduate courses in modern poetry and literary criticism. She was chairman of the English Department 1969–1972. Professor Hénault earned her B.A. and M.A. degrees at the University of Washington in Seattle and her Ph.D. from the University of Maryland in College Park, Maryland.

Dr. Hénault has published articles on Henry James and J. F. Powers in *American Literature* and *America*; books on Peter Viereck (Twayne Publishers); and Ezra Pound (Charles E. Merrill Publishers); and is also a published writer of short stories.

An organizer and one of the three co-directors of "Women and Society: A Symposium," a three-day, multi-disciplinary, international conference held at Saint Michael's College, Dr. Hénault read a paper there at that time on the image of the widow in American literature, March 23, 1979.

Preface

Published now for fifty years, the poems of Stanley Kunitz have won for him awards and fellowships and prizes, including a Pulitzer in 1959, the Consultantship in Poetry to the Library of Congress in 1974 and 1975, election to the fifty-member American Academy of Arts and Letters in 1975, and the Chancellorship of the Academy of American Poets. He has had as well words of praise from poets and critics and reviewers; he has been interviewed for literary journals many times; yet his work has still not had any wide critical attention. A principal aim of this book is to establish the excellence and importance of Kunitz's poetry. To do this I outline and assess his accomplishment, describe the special qualities of his verse, and single out for close examination some of his best poems.

Hence Chapter 1 gives the essential biographical facts. Chapters 2 and 3 enumerate his themes, forms and techniques; Chapter 4 interlinks his first books of poetry and discusses their "interior logics" and characteristics. Chapter 5 concerns his 1971 and 1974 books of poetry, *The Testing-Tree* and *The Terrible Threshold*; 6, his translations of Russian poets, particularly Anna Akhmatova. Chapter 7 surveys his 1975 collection of prose writings, and the Conclusion summarizes and evaluates Kunitz's work of fifty years.

Of Kunitz's five books of original poetry only *Selected Poems* and *The Testing-Tree* were in print in the United States at the time I was writing this book, and for the text of the poems from the first two books, *Intellectual Things* and *Passport to the War*, whenever possible I cite from *Selected Poems. Poems of Stanley Kunitz, 1928–1978* was published after this manuscript was set in type and could not be considered here.

An outstanding critical fact about Stanley Kunitz's poetry is that, though distinguished, it has not so far received the recognition that it merits. Some reasons for this neglect are alluded to in the pages that follow; nonetheless in general I have eschewed exploring this problem in any detail because the vagaries of the literary stock market are such that even as I write the circumstances no doubt are changing. Some evidence that this might be so is that while I was working on this book, literary journals published interviews with him about his poetry and the *New York Times Magazine* featured an article about his gardens and their relationship to his poetry. In addition the publication of his Akhmatova translation and his prose book, *A Kind of Order, A Kind of Folly*, and his 1974 and 1975 appointments as Consultant in Poetry to the Library of Congress stirred up some interest in him and in his work. Kunitz's selection of his poems for a British audience theretofore unfamiliar with his poetry, *The Terrible Threshold: Selected Poems, 1940-1970*, published in 1974, too, was favorably and widely reviewed in England. It is my expectation that the July 1979 publication of his *Poems of Stanley Kunitz 1928-1978* by Atlantic-Little, Brown will remind the whole of the literary establishment of how good a poet Stanley Kunitz is and has been for half a century.

Yet no book other than this one has been yet written about Kunitz's work; each of his peers—Robert Lowell, Theodore Roethke, Richard Eberhart, and Richard Wilbur—has had at least a volume devoted to his work alone. Further, the critical articles on Kunitz's poetry are few. Besides the some half-dozen listed in the Selected Bibliography, comments on his work are confined to reviews of his books and scattered passages in books on twentieth-century poetry. Kunitz's poetry is known—but not fully enough. Asked in 1967 why he thought Kunitz was neglected, W. H. Auden remarked that it *was* "strange, but give him time. A hundred years or so. He's a patient man. He won't mind waiting." *Would* he mind waiting? Kunitz was asked later. "No. I've waited a good many years. I can wait—a hundred more."[1]

The 1975 critical discussion of Kunitz's work in *World Authors*, a reference work for which he acted as editorial consultant, said that "critics seeking to explain this neglect pointed out that he writes slowly and rejects much, that his work is condensed and sometimes hermetic and sometimes painful, probing too deeply for comfort into the human psyche."[2] Yet when, around that same time, he was queried about one critic's observation that he has "remained a poet's poet, without readers," Kunitz vigorously answered that "fortunately" it was "not true!" that he had no readers.[3] A further consideration may be the one he touches on in an imaginary dialogue that he wrote the year he won the Pulitzer Prize (1959); there Kunitz had called attention to the "distinguished poets [who] have remained relatively obscure for years, even for decades, either through anthological caprice or simply because their work did not seem to lend itself to captivity in the standard zoos of the period."[4] Both of these—"anthological caprice" and the uniqueness of his poetry—may have worked to make Kunitz, in John Ciardi's words of 1958, "certainly the most neglected good poet of the last quarter-century." For that is the hard fact that makes a discussion of Kunitz's "neglect" necessary—he is a "good poet," an excellent poet.

Yet, as he pointed out in 1960, "The great lack is not poets but readers." For, he continued,

Poetry speaks to the best in us, whereas we live in an age where the second-best, the good-enough, is king. Popularity is not to be expected for an art that is bitten by the ideal.[5]

Indeed, as Kunitz said in another essay, "Most poets bear with remarkable grace their inability to attract mobs of readers; what infuriates them is the ignorant assumption that their unpopularity is to be attributed to the irrelevance or frivolity of what they have to say."[6] Kunitz's art, "bitten by the ideal," is both relevant and serious, as has been noted by reputable and important poets and critics who rank him high, as they should.

For one, the formal qualities in his early poetry—meter, rhyme, image, stanza—raise it above the ordinary; in Richard Wilbur's words, "Kunitz has every technical virtue." Then the later poetry, that of the 1960s and 1970s, freer and simpler, as Robert Lowell has said, "unencumbered and trustful," still maintains a hard line. Overall while Kunitz's poetry is intellectual and learned, its content based on such sciences as psychology and astronomy, it is not, early and late, the highly allusive, cryptic, bookish poetry of a Pound or an Eliot, but rather a personal, emotional, disciplined poetry uniquely his own, separated from fads and fashions.

Writing in the late 1920s, early 1930s, and on into the 1970s, Stanley Kunitz consistently went his own way, meticulous in craft, spare in publication, and seemingly unaffected by what other poets might have been doing. Moreover, though, as T. S. Eliot observed, "art never improves," an individual artist can improve and often does, and the poems of Kunitz's late sixties and early seventies have lines and effects that one could not have predicted while reading the earlier poetry. A 1951 poem like "The Waltzer in the House," for instance, a middle-period poem, is a charming lyric in praise of a mouse, "A little blossom of a beast. . . ."[7] The dramatic situation is that a newly wed lady

> . . . feeds him tarts and curds,
> Seeds packaged for the birds,
> And figs, and nuts, and cheese . . . ,

and the mouse dances for her. The repetition of "sweet," "delicate," "swaying," "bobbing" in the twenty-one short lines of the poem, the easy musical rhyme ("beast-yeast," "trance-dance"), and the light mood make "The Waltzer in the House" a little like a rondeau or a ballade, though it is neither, and a delightful poem altogether.

In contrast, "Robin Redbreast," from *The Testing-Tree* (pp. 22–23), a poem published eighteen years later, is an implacably hard poem with cold, precise imagery and no embellishment of rhyme or meter, a moment in life at its flaying worst. The action here is the persona's rescuing of a robin from some "tormenting" jays. The robin is

> . . . the dingiest bird
> you ever saw, all the color
> washed from him, as if
> he had been standing in the rain,
> friendless and stiff and cold,
> since Eden went wrong.

"Poor thing! Poor foolish life!" the "I" says of him; "without sense enough to stop," the bird had been

> running in desperate circles,
> needing my lucky help
> to toss him back into his element.
> But when I held him high,
> fear clutched my hand,
> for through the hole in his head,
> cut whistle-clean . . .
> through the old dried wound
> between his eyes
> where the hunter's brand
> had tunneled out his wits . . .
> I caught the cold flash of the blue
> unappeasable sky.

(ellipses in text)

Both of these poems, like Kunitz's others, are exquisitely finished, fine in diction, firm in form. The second one, characteristically, is a profound probing of life's pain, ineluctably Kunitzian. Thus, while Kunitz's poems are not numerous, taken altogether they make up an important body of work of considerable power and originality.

MARIE HÉNAULT

St. Michael's College

Acknowledgments

My first acknowledgment is to my late husband, Robert J. Hénault, formerly of the St. Michael's College History Department, to whom this book is dedicated. He eliminated many infelicities in the early drafts of this book, accompanied me on a trip to Provincetown to meet and talk with Stanley Kunitz, and did countless other things of which page after page of this book are reminders. His death on May 8, 1978, deprived me of much more than his constant and considerable editorial help; his interest and presence were important forces in all my past work.

Stanley Kunitz sent me books and manuscripts throughout the years of preparation, was of great assistance to me in arriving at permission agreements, and in many letters and in person kindly answered many questions and solved some problems. My debt to him, incalculable, is beyond words, and I thank him here with all my heart.

My St. Michael's College colleagues I thank for assistance of many kinds, large and small; listing them alphabetically I thank warmly Armand Citarella, Nick Clary, Paul Couture, John Engels, George Lahage, Edward Murphy, and John Reiss.

I thank also Mary Rivard, St. Michael's College Reference Librarian, who tirelessly helped me to find and acquire materials and was ever on the alert for references that might be of help to me.

Donovan McDonough I thank for many different kinds of help— for careful readings of the manuscript, for information, discussion, good taste, fine judgment, and invaluable friendship.

Michael Martinsen, a student in the first of the classes with whom I read Kunitz's poetry, I owe special thanks to also. He wrote a paper on Kunitz's poetry for that 1971 class at my suggestion and showed me the possibilities of a study like this one; for long he continued to be interested in Kunitz and in my work on this book. His too early death in February 1978 I record here.

I thank, too, each one of the students in my Spring 1975 course in Twentieth Century Poetry who contributed in one way or another to my understanding of and writing about Kunitz's poetry—Michael Campbell, Sara Dillon, Ronald Gagnon, Peter Keefe, Kipp Miller, and Kevin Rita. In addition, one of them, Ronald Gagnon, assisted me in the late stages of my research with enthusiasm and industry, ascertaining facts that greatly enrich my text. I thank him for proofreading, also, and, most of all, for exuberant discussion that encouraged me to complete an early version of my manuscript months before I might otherwise have done so.

St. Michael's College itself gave me a grant to help in my expenses, but more than that supplied the atmosphere, the moral support and trust necessary when a manuscript is worked on and talked about for years and only at last produced.

Susan Dunn, a 1979 St. Michael's graduate, gave generously of her time, energy, persistence, and intelligence to make the final manuscript text as accurate a one as it could possibly be. I thank her heartily and wish her well in all her endeavors.

My friends and colleagues Carey Kaplan and Buff Lindau, my son, Martial, my daughter-in-law, Jeannette, and my two grandchildren, Theresa Marie and Heather Joyce, I thank also for being what they are and for being around. The book is as good a piece of work as I can make it at this time, and all my thanks do not mean that anyone other than myself is responsible for any lapses in fact, judgment, or taste.

Kunitz quotations are given by permission of Atlantic-Little, Brown and Stanley Kunitz.

Chronology

1905 July 29, born in Worcester, Massachusetts, one of three children (two sisters) of Solomon Z. Kunitz and Yetta (Jasspon) Kunitz.

1926 A.B., Harvard University, *summa cum laude.*

1927 A.M., Harvard University.

1928– Edited *Wilson Library Bulletin* and Wilson reference books,
1943 H. W. Wilson Company, New York City.

1929– Lived in France and Italy.
1930

1930 Published *Intellectual Things*, first book of poetry. Married Helen Pearce. Moved to Wormwood Hill, Mansfield Center, Connecticut.

1933 Edited *Living Authors: A Book of Biographies*, for the H. W. Wilson Company. Edited, with Howard Haycraft and Wilbur C. Hadden, *Authors Today and Yesterday. A Companion Volume to Living Authors.*

1934 Edited, with Howard Haycraft, *The Junior Book of Authors.*

1936 Edited, with Howard Haycraft, *British Authors of the Nineteenth Century.*

1937 Divorced from Helen Pearce. Moved to Lingan Green, New Hope, Bucks County, Pennsylvania.

1938 Edited, with Howard Haycraft, *American Authors, 1600–1900.*

1939 Married Eleanor Evans.

1941 Received the Oscar Blumenthal Prize, *Poetry* Magazine.

1942 Edited, with Howard Haycraft, *Twentieth Century Authors.*

1943– Served in the United States Army with the Air Transport
1945 Command: noncommissioned officer in charge of information and education; private to staff sergeant.

1944 Published *Passport to the War*, second book of poetry.

1945– Awarded John Simon Guggenheim Memorial fellowship.
1946 Resided in Santa Fe, New Mexico.

1946– Taught at Bennington College, Bennington, Vermont.
1949

1949– Taught at Potsdam State Teachers College, Potsdam, New
1950   York.

1949– Directed seminar, Potsdam Summer Workshop in Creative
1953   Arts, Potsdam, New York.

1950   Birth of daughter, Gretchen.

1950– Taught at the New School for Social Research, New York
1958   City.

1952   Edited, with Howard Haycraft, *British Authors Before 1800.*

1953– Received Amy Lowell Travelling Fellowship. Lived in Italy
1954   and France.

1955   Edited, with Vineta Colby, *Twentieth Century Authors. First
       Supplement.*

1955– Appointed poet-in-residence, University of Washington,
1956   Seattle, Washington.

1956   Received Levinson Prize, *Poetry* magazine.

1956– Appointed poet-in-residence, Queens College, New York
1957   City.

1957   Received *Saturday Review* award. Began summer residence in
       Provincetown, Cape Cod, Massachusetts.

1958   Divorced from Eleanor Evans. Married Elise Asher. Received
       Harriet Monroe Award, University of Chicago. Published
       Selected Poems, third book of poetry. Received Fellowship
       Award, Academy of American Poets.

1958– Appointed poet-in-residence, Brandeis University, Waltham,
1959   Massachusetts. Received Ford Foundation grant.

1958– Directed Poetry Workshop of the Poetry Center, Young
1962   Men's Hebrew Association, New York City.

1959   Awarded Pulitzer Prize for *Selected Poems.* Received Na-
       tional Institute of Arts and Letters award.

1961   Received Honorary Doctor of Letters degree, Clark Univer-
       sity, Worcester, Massachusetts.

1961– Served as Danforth Visiting Lecturer at colleges and univer-
1963   sities in the United States.

1963– to the present. Appointed lecturer at Columbia University,
       School of General Studies, New York City; since 1967 adjunct
       professor of writing in the School of the Arts, Columbia
       University. Selected as one of 250 members of the National
       Institute of Arts and Letters.

1964   Edited *Poems of John Keats.*

1965 Received Brandeis University Medal of Achievement.
1967 Translated, with others, *Antiworlds and the Fifth Ace*, by Andrei Voznesensky. Edited, with Vineta Colby, *European Authors, 1000-1900*.
1968 Received Fellowship Award, Academy of American Poets.
1968– to the present. Helped organize and for part of the year serves as member of staff of writing division, Fine Arts Work Center, Provincetown, Massachusetts.
1969– Edited Yale Series of Younger Poets, Yale University Press.
1977 Appointed Fellow, Yale University.
1970 Taught as visiting lecturer, Yale University. Elected Chancellor, Academy of American Poets.
1971 Published *The Testing-Tree*, fourth book of poetry.
1973 Translated, with Max Hayward, *Poems of Anna Akhmatova*.
1974 Appointed twenty-third Consultant in Poetry to the Library of Congress. Published *The Terrible Threshold*, a selection of poems for British readers. Translated, with others, *Story Under Full Sail* by Andrei Voznesensky.
1975 Published *A Kind of Order, A Kind of Folly: Essays and Conversations*, prose book. Reappointed Consultant in Poetry to the Library of Congress. Elected to the fifty-member American Academy of Arts and Letters, succeeding to the Chair held by John Crowe Ransom. Editorial Consultant, *World Authors, 1950-1970* (ed. by John Wakeman), a companion to *Twentieth Century Authors* (1942) and *Twentieth Century Authors. First Supplement* (1955).
1976 Lectured and read on a tour to the West Coast of Africa.
1978 Edited and acted as co-translator of *Orchard Lamps* by Ukrainian poet Ivan Drach.
1978 Senior Fellow in the Humanities at Princeton University teaching creative writing for one term.
1979 *The Poems of Stanley Kunitz, 1928-1978*, sixth book of poetry.

CHAPTER 1

Introduction

BORN in Worcester, Massachusetts, in 1905, Stanley Kunitz came of age after the first skirmishes of the moderns and the traditionalists were over. In 1922, the year of the publication of the two landmark works of the moderns, *The Waste Land* and *Ulysses*, Kunitz was seventeen and valedictorian of his class at Worcester Classical High School. He won a scholarship to Harvard University, from which he earned an A.B. in English in 1926, *summa cum laude,* and an M.A. in 1927. "At Harvard," he has written, he "pronounced [himself] an advocate of the Moderns, from Hopkins down to Joyce and Eliot and Cummings." For his Master's thesis he examined their "techniques . . . much to the consternation of my triumvirate of mentors, Professors Lowes and Kittredge and Babbitt."[1]

In his summers Kunitz had been serving an apprenticeship on the *Worcester Telegram*, and after college he became a reporter and feature writer for that publication. One of the stories that he reported that "left a mark" on him, he has written, was that of the Sacco-Vanzetti trial of 1927. "Their case became my cause," he continues, "and shortly after their executions in August 1927 I left for New York on a mission to find a publisher for Vanzetti's letters." Their eventual publication many years later, without Kunitz's "intervention," was a contrast to the reaction to them in publishing circles in 1927.[2]

In New York City Kunitz went to work for the H. W. Wilson Company, a publishing house with which he remained associated, though largely in absentia, through the 1930s and into the 1940s. It was his first important job and the one that he held the longest. For the Wilson Company Kunitz edited their house journal, the *Wilson Bulletin for Librarians*, and contributed to it a monthly column entitled at first "Dilly Tante Observes." Kunitz's own name began appearing on the masthead in January 1935; when, under his direction, the publication was renamed the *Wilson Library Bulletin* in September 1939, the column became "The Roving Eye" and was signed with his own initials.[3]

Librarian Jesse Shera gives testimony to what Kunitz accomplished here: "To our full buoyancy of youth, the *Wilson Library Bulletin* gave a generous share of hope, and joy, and aspiration. . . . With Stanley Kunitz at its head, it was a rallying point for a group of youngsters who were in hot revolt against tradition."[4] Transforming this house publication into "something a great deal more stimulating and socially conscious than the house organ it was intended to be"[5] was only a part of Kunitz's work for the H. W. Wilson Company; he also edited nine biographical dictionaries, mostly with Howard Haycraft, beginning with *Living Authors: A Book of Biographies* in 1933. *Authors Today and Yesterday* followed, as did *The Junior Book of Authors* in 1934 and *British Authors of the Nineteenth Century* in 1936, and so on through five other volumes, including *European Authors, 1000–1900*, with Vineta Colby, in 1967. For the 1975 Wilson volume *World Authors, 1950–1970*, edited by John Wakeman, Kunitz served as editorial consultant.

These works which Kunitz helped edit between 1933 and 1975 must be part of his bibliography. Making his name widely known among librarians and researchers, these fat books are pioneer work in the field of biographical compilation and collection. So useful for ready and reasonably accurate information about their title subjects, "living authors," "American authors, 1600–1900," "twentieth century authors," it seems caviling to single out, as some reviewers have, omissions, occasional inaccuracies, perpetuation of myths, or mistruths. The sheer monumentality of these works and the largeness of the need that they fill make extensive adverse criticism seem mere quibbling.

This editing was done, of course, as Kunitz has said, "simply" because he "had to earn a living,"[6] and so these thousands of pages are his journey work only. His poetry, so much less in bulk, is unquestionably more significant. Hence I mention these reference works here and then also list them in the Chronology and in the Selected Bibliography but shall not consider them further.

"Even in grade school I was rhyming," Kunitz has recalled, "doggerel, mainly."[7] And, although Harvard (in his later sardonic estimation) was "a great place" for *discouraging* poets, a visiting professor of composition there, Robert Gay, told him, "You are a poet—be one."[8] Kunitz began to write, he has said, in order to discover as poets perennially have, "who I was, what I stood for, how I stood in relation to the world around me."[9] At Harvard he won the coveted Lloyd McKim Garrison Medal for Poetry; after college he began publishing his poems in magazines. In 1929 and 1930 several appeared in *Poetry* magazine, *Commonweal*, the *New Republic*, the *Nation*, and in the *Dial* under Marianne Moore's editorship. About the latter Kunitz has noted that the "biggest thrill" of this time was a letter in Marianne Moore's "spidery hand" accepting his poems. Just out of college he felt that he "had been blessed by the gods."[10]

In 1930 Doubleday, Doran published Kunitz's first book of poems, *Intellectual Things*. In the next year he began regularly to review books of verse for *Poetry*, and he continued to do so through 1942. After his war service he wrote some more reviews for *Poetry*, some for the *Nation* and the *New Republic*, and several for *Harper's*, but after the early 1960s he no longer contributed reviews frequently to journals. Book reviews, too, can be a writer's journey work; Kunitz's forty or fifty reviews extending over a period of three decades are, however, a compendium of discriminating judgments and wise statements about the art of poetry that aspiring poets and critics might still find useful. A selection from these and from his other prose writings make up his 1975 book, *A Kind of Order, A Kind of Folly: Essays and Conversations*.[11]

"To tell the true artist from the false is one of the responsibilities of criticism," Kunitz wrote in 1960,[12] and from 1969 to 1977 some of this work of discrimination and judgment, telling the true artist from the false, continued in his work as editor and judge for the Yale Series of Younger Poets. In 1970 to the *New York Quarterly* interviewer he said that this meant "reading some 500 book-length manuscripts a year" (later increased to 750). And he actually tried, too, he added, "to read every one of them, though not necessarily every page . . . a responsibility" he refused to "unload on others, because—who knows?—the most miraculous, most original work of all might get weeded out in the first round." Finally, however, he said, "It becomes clear that there are only three or four manuscripts, maybe, in the lot from which any sort of fire breaks each time you turn to them."[13] In reading these manuscripts he was not looking "for any specific kind of poet. . . . I'm looking for a poet. Let me add that nobody has an inside track. All but one of the poets I've picked have been perfect strangers."[14] When he got to the finalists, the last three or four manuscripts from which "fire breaks," he wished "the rules of the game didn't require me to make an arbitrary choice." For, Kunitz concluded, as Blake said, "'I cannot think that Real Poets have any competition. None are greatest in the Kingdom of Heaven.'"[15]

When Kunitz was drafted into the army in 1943 during World War II, he was in his late thirties, a published poet and writer. As a conscientious objector he "had accepted service," he has said, "on the promise that I would not bear arms, but the Army refused to acknowledge the terms of our agreement. . . ." The result was "a nightmare from beginning to end."[16] Entering as a private he was discharged as a staff sergeant after serving as a noncommissioned officer in charge of information and education, editing a weekly army news magazine called *Ten Minute Break*. For a while he had thought that he might be able to continue with at least one part of his civilian life, writing his column "The Roving Eye" for the *Wilson Library Bulletin*. In May 1943, a short time after his induction, he confessed that he was "so deeply immersed in this new, curious life of mine that I have had to let nearly all my contacts with the outside world go by the board. . . . To continue with 'The Roving Eye' is out of the question for the present."[17]

In the years since 1930 when his first book of poetry, *Intellectual Things*, had appeared, Kunitz had published poems, mostly in *Poetry* but also in the *Nation*, the *Saturday Review of Literature*, the *American Mercury*, and other journals. In 1944 many of these poems along with an almost equal number from the out-of-print *Intellectual Things* were collected into a second volume of poems, *Passport to the War*. Some of Kunitz's best and best-known poems are new in this book: "My Surgeons" and "Father and Son," to cite examples, all led off by one of his excellent "war" poems, "Reflection by a Mailbox." In that latter poem, Kunitz wrote that he waited

> . . . under the hemlock by the road
> For the red-haired postman with the smiling hand
> To bring me my passport to the war.   (SP, 94)

The war for him was another country, his "darkest time."[18] And for him, also, as for many men of his generation and that younger, the rest of his life had to be temporarily in hiatus—not only writing "The Roving Eye" but also reviewing books and writing poems. The "cruel age . . . deflected" him, in the words of his translation of an Akhmatova poem, "like a river from its course."[19]

After his war service he held a Guggenheim Fellowship for a year (1945–1946), living in Santa Fe, and then at the prompting and insistence of his friend Theodore Roethke he went to Bennington College in Vermont to teach. As Kunitz tells it, while he was still in the army he had been offered the position, seemingly "out of nowhere. . . . I snatched at it. . . . I knew that Roethke was at Bennington, but didn't know that he had been through a violent manic episode—one of his worst. They wanted to ease him out, but he was being difficult about it. Finally, he told them he would leave quietly on one condition: hire Kunitz. So that's how I began teaching." [20]

Kunitz began his teaching at Bennington, then, in 1946, nearly twenty years after he had earned his Master's degree at Harvard. At that time, 1927, he had expected to be offered a teaching appointment, "not because I was already a poet but because of my scholarship record." As one of the less pleasant aspects of the times, he notes, that he "was told indirectly through the head of the English department that Anglo-Saxons would resent being taught English by a Jew, even a Jew with a *summa cum laude*. That shook my world," Kunitz said. "It seemed to me such a cruel and wanton rejection that I turned away from the academic world completely." [21]

This "turning away," then, continued for nearly twenty years, and by the time he began at Bennington in 1946 he was in his early forties, a late start for any academic career. He remained there for three years and afterwards taught at many other colleges and universities, the State University of New York at Potsdam, the New School for Social Research, the University of Washington, and others. He did so, though, he has said, "on a year-to-year basis, without tenure." When he began what became his longtime association with Columbia University in 1963, he maintained his "freedom" by signing only a one-year contract and did not accept tenure. An "adjunct professor, attached to the graduate school of writing," he taught, he said, for the students, not the institution. [22]

When asked by young poets if they should become teachers, Kunitz tried to discourage them. "On the whole I think it's stultifying for young poets to leap immediately into the academic life," he explained. "They would be better off testing the rigors of a less regulated existence. I was over 40 when I began to teach, and I am grateful now for the difficult years of my preparation. And I still consider myself a free agent. . . ." [23]

The importance and value of Kunitz's own teaching to them is evidenced by poets now publishing who list study with him at Columbia as an essential part of their training. For himself, coming to it "late" he "found it second nature."[24] How did he teach the writing of poetry? "Thoroughly," he said. "Passionately. Long ago," he added, "I discarded theories. The danger of the poet-as-teacher lies in his imposing his *persona* on his students. I welcome any kind of poet; I don't care if he is my kind or not. Some of the best students I've worked with have turned out to be my own opposites."[25]

What he tried to do, Kunitz said, "is to help each person rediscover the poet within himself." He said "rediscover," he continued, "because I am convinced that it is a universal human attribute to want to play with words, to beat out rhythms, to fashion images, to tell a story, to construct forms. . . ." Everyone has the "key" to doing this "in his possession: what prevents him from using it is mainly inertia, the stultification of the senses as a result of our one-sided educational conditioning and the fear of being made ridiculous or ashamed by the exposure of his feelings."[26] Besides that, "our heads [are] . . . full of the day's clatter. The task is to get through to the other side, where we can hear the deep rhythms that connect us with the stars and the tides."[27] This last element, "periodicity," he said, "is what gives us the sense of a universal pulse. And any art that does not convey that sense is a lesser art."[28]

In 1958 Kunitz's third book of poems, *Selected Poems*, was brought out by Atlantic, Little, Brown, who remained his publishers, succeeding Doubleday, Doran for the first book and Henry Holt for the second. The publication of this Pulitzer Prize–winning volume, Kunitz has said, was attended with difficulty, three publishers refusing to read the manuscript and five rejecting it. Containing eighty-five poems, thirty-five of them new, a longer book than either of his other two, *Selected Poems* included many of the best poems from the first two volumes and notable new ones such as the opening and closing pieces, "The Science of the Night" and "A Spark of Laurel." It also brought Stanley Kunitz to the attention of critics and readers, and was reviewed in all the major journals and greatly praised.

John Ciardi, for instance, wrote, "Kunitz is certainly the most neglected good poet of the last quarter-century," and Robert Lowell commented that Kunitz had "been one of the masters for years, and yet so unrecognized that his *Selected Poems* make him the poet of the hour." Vivian Mercier thought that "if the quantity of [Kunitz's] output catches up with its quality, we may yet learn to rank him among the great American poets of this century."[29] Certainly quantity alone does not make a great poet or a great writer; still, along with high quality it seems a requirement for the truly great among our literary figures. Commenting on this, Kunitz said that he "realize[d] that reputations are made by volume as much as by anything else. Most of the big reputations in modern American poetry have been made on the basis of a large body of work." However, "That doesn't happen to be my style," he added. "Over a lifetime I've written poems only when I felt I had poems to write. . . ."[30]

As, in Lowell's phrase, "the poet of the hour," Kunitz won the Pulitzer Prize for Poetry in 1959 and also received the National Institute of Arts and Letters grant in poetry. At this time, too, he was one of the first group of eleven writers to be given a two-year Ford Foundation grant designed to "give artists at the peak of their creative lives the freedom to concentrate on their work without interruption from side activities."[31]

The fourteen-year intervals between the dates of Kunitz's first three books, 1930, 1944, and 1958, suggested that symmetrically his fourth book would be published in 1972. Instead, it came out a year "early," in 1971, and revealed a new, freer Kunitz experimenting with looser forms, a shorter line, and delving into subjects not previously much dealt with: recollections from early childhood ("The Magic Curtain," "The Portrait"); analogies from nature ("King of the River"); politics ("Around Pastor Bonhoeffer"); and others. *The Testing-Tree*, with thirty poems, fewer than in any of his other three books, concludes with three pages of "Notes," explanatory, illuminating, autobiographical, and also necessary information about the twenty-three original poems and the seven translations included. These last poems found their way into the book, Kunitz said, because he "liked them as poems. And because they seemed to have an affinity with my own work."[32]

Six of the seven translated poems in *The Testing-Tree* are from the Russian. For an event important in Kunitz's literary biography is his friendship with the Russian poet Andrei Voznesensky which resulted, he said, in a rediscovery of his "own Russian ancestry, which I had almost forgotten. . . . Suddenly I felt close to Russian poetry, as though I had been waiting to hear it for years."[33] When he visited Russia in 1967 as part of the Cultural Exchange Program, he "became deeply involved in the lives and fates of her poets." Of these,

Kunitz said, Anna "Akhmatova's pure and unaffected voice [had] . . . the kind of speech" he valued. "I think I can learn from her. That's as good a reason as any for trying to translate her." [34]

The translation of Akhmatova, "one of the great figures of modern Russian poetry" (TT, 67), occupied Kunitz for years. His edition of her poems was published in the summer of 1973, and along with three other books—*The Terrible Threshold*, a selection of his poems for a British public; *Story Under Full Sail*, a translation of a dramatic poem by Andrei Voznesensky; and *A Kind of Order, A Kind of Folly*, a prose volume—gave Kunitz four books in three years, a change from his previous slimness of output. "The anomaly," as Kunitz said, "is that, as one of the few survivors of my generation of poets, I'm suddenly threatening to become prolific—for me, that is." [35] In 1974 a long-overdue honor came with Kunitz's appointment as twenty-third Consultant in Poetry to the Library of Congress, the most prestigious post available to a poet in the United States. In 1975 he was reappointed for a second term.

I   *Quality of Voice and Mind*

As a final biographical note we can ask, What are Kunitz's poetic roots? To which earlier poets is he most indebted? Whose poetry is his most like? These questions of "influence" are usually not easy ones to answer. But Kunitz was quite open about "influences" on his work and development, another result, possibly, of his being a "survivor" of his generation of poets, and so these can be listed and succinctly discussed without the necessity of quoting lines or citing poems as evidence. Despite the number of "influences" on his work, Kunitz still had his own "quality of voice and mind," as will be shown in the following chapters.

Who, then, were some of the poets of importance to Kunitz? Baudelaire, he said, is one, and Rimbaud. Then, Hopkins, who "overwhelmed" him in his college years. Donne and Herbert influenced him "stylistically." He was, he said, "mad about the metaphysical poets," and since in his time in college, "There wasn't even a course in the metaphysical poets . . . I came upon them independently, and they seemed closest to that particular quality of voice and mind that I cared about . . . historically the way into the new poetry was through the doorway of the seventeenth century, through the rediscovery of the metaphysical tradition."

As other past poets important to him, Kunitz also named Herrick—Martin Post, his high-school English teacher, recited "one of Robert Herrick's songs" in class and "changed [his] life"—Marvell, and Milton. Kunitz's phrasing and diction here and there are mildly Miltonic, but little is so definite that one can point directly to specific instances of debts to this great seventeenth-century poet. In the next century, William Blake, who influenced his poetry, Kunitz said, "prophetically," differs from other previous poets by being so pervasive an influence on Kunitz's early poetry that the subject is discussed at more length later. Aside from Blake no other poet of the eighteenth century seems to have had an effect on Kunitz's work.

Other poets whom Kunitz singles out are "Keats, Tennyson, Wordsworth"; they, along with Blake, are "the poets who shook" him. When he was in high school, he said, "a neighbor gave me Wordsworth's collected poems," and this was a "red-letter day." From Wordsworth's "Prelude" and "Intimations of Immortality," Kunitz commented, he thought that he "must have learned something. . . ." And, for a while, he "steeped" himself in Keats and Tennyson. At Harvard he studied with John Livingston Lowes, whose "faith was in the Romantic poets," as was Kunitz's, too. Yeats, though, he said, he considered "to be the great master of the poem in English in this century."

Of the two other outstanding figures in early twentieth-century poetry in English, T. S. Eliot and Ezra Pound, Kunitz said that "they had no reputation in the academic or general world" when he began to write. To be born in his generation, though, Kunitz went on to say, "is to have been born in the shadow of the great names who belonged to the previous generation. . . ." Thus he supposed that he was influenced by

. . . Eliot, to a degree, though I opposed him, quarreling with his ideas, his criticism, and what I thought of as his poverty of sympathy. His theory of the depersonalization of poetry struck me as false and destructive. My work didn't fit into that picture of his at all.

Both Kunitz and Theodore Roethke, his one literary friend early in his career, "felt from the beginning," Kunitz said, "that the Eliot school was our principal adversary. We fought for a more passionate art. Nevertheless I was so aware of his existence that even in a negative way I was influenced by him. . . . That Eliot rhythm has an hypnotic effect." Pound, one gathers, was no influence at all, except

possibly on Kunitz's theory of translation. In Kunitz's view Pound is an "inventor" among the poets, a lesser poet than Yeats, and Yeats, in his opinion, may "in the long run . . . prove to be more influential." [36]
From this catalogue we can cite as probably most important Baudelaire, Hopkins, Blake, and Yeats. And I would include also Wordsworth's great contemporary Coleridge, the principal study of John Livingston Lowes, Kunitz's teacher at Harvard. Though Kunitz alludes to Coleridge only once in his poems, the form and content of some of his poems, as noted later, are quite like those of Coleridge's "conversation poems," and surely he "learned" from him as he did from the other poets that he generously named as influences. [37]

CHAPTER 2

The Fable of My Life

"THE mature poet is self-defining," Stanley Kunitz declared in his middle years. "It is as though," he wrote,

> . . . having drawn a circle round himself at sufficient radius to encompass the critical phenomena of our experience, he had said: "This is the field of my adventure, which I shall explore implacably, identifying all my population with name and number, assigning to each beast, each man, each god therein a useful part in the fable of my life."[1]

Thirty years later, in 1972, he said simply "that the effort is to convert one's life into legend. . . ."[2] The truth of this even a casual reading of Kunitz's poetry substantiates. Primarily, archetypal patterns are used, though terms and images recur, too. Most often this is oblique, not direct, with "The Way Down" (SP, 106–108) a rare exception in its deliberate archetypal terminology—the title itself, for instance. Furthermore, not only in imagery and diction but also in form, content, and theme all of Kunitz's poems bear his signature; in words from Shakespeare, "every word doth almost tell my name." Until the late 1950s his poems were mostly in traditional forms, a sonnet or two, couplets, rhymed quatrains, and long meditative poems in blank-verse paragraphs. "Revolving Meditation," the last but one poem in *Selected Poems*, is for Kunitz a "bridge poem" marking a shift away from strict metrical adherence toward the later characteristic "functional stressing."

All of Kunitz's poems, though, early and late, are lyrical, personal, emotional, and intense. None of his poems is public or occasional like Robert Lowell's "Quaker Graveyard at Nantucket" or "For the Union Dead." Reading Kunitz, rather, one comes to know the persona of the poet and his feelings about the "fable" of his life, though still not in the personally identifiable, anguished way one does

29

in the poetry of such "confessional" poets as Lowell himself (in his nonpublic aspect) or Anne Sexton or Sylvia Plath.

For Kunitz is not at all a confessional poet, and most likely he would himself, too, as he said about Roethke, "vomit . . . at the thought" of being called one. As he said, "Secrets are part of the legend," the "fable" of his life. And his own "emphasis isn't on spilling everything." [3] Hence, although he writes about himself in the main, he by no means tells "all." Neither, on the other hand, are the figures that march through his poems masks or objective creations, the Tiresiases, Odysseuses, Prufrocks, Mauberleys, Crazy Janes, Catherines, or Kavanaughs of Eliot, Pound, Yeats, and Lowell.

Like theirs, of course, some of his poetry is allusive, but not greatly so. Allusions, particularly those to the classical tradition, are rather much a well-read poet's stock in trade—especially in his youth. And so some of Kunitz's poems make references to various mythic persons, places, objects, and events: Oedipus, Odysseus, Agamemnon, Clytemnestra, Apollo, Zeus; Thebes, Point Lotus, Lethe; golden bough, laurel, and shower of gold—among others. Most of these do not seem to be obscure, are not central, and would appear to be used principally to recall eternally true stories and motifs.

In Kunitz's poetry such allusions become rarer as he turned his own life into fable and found therein such mythic parallels as the "Lilith" woman in "The Dark and the Fair" and the lost father in "Father and Son." Both of these take on archetypal lineaments, though they are grounded firmly, it seems, in experience and in the poet's examination of his own life.

For, as Kunitz noted in 1968, "Every poet has his own idiosyncrasies, . . . his own . . . central sources, his own pastness which is different from any other poet. . . ." The "originality of any poet," he continued, "consists to a considerable degree in finding those key images which forever haunt him, which make him different from others."[4] In Kunitz's poetry the single most important figure is certainly his own persona, a Self which speaks in something very like Kunitz's own voice, single and solitary, guilt-ridden, pain-wracked and compassionate. Others are the Beloved Woman and the Father, each in about three incarnations. In addition are a Christ, a Roman thief, a Magus, the devil, the Bitch, the Masked Man, the old clothes man, the man upstairs and in the park—and, finally, a few allegorical personages, Disorder, Phantoms, phobias, surgeons.

I *The Beloved Woman*

Among Kunitz's subjects for poems are love, man's nature, time, the mind, death, the Self, a yearning for the lost father, regret, sorrow, disillusionment, and many other traditional emotions and moods. Love is the most frequent and the most important and the most complicated of these subjects. In his view when poets no longer write love poetry they would do "better [to] turn to prose." For "All poetry," he said, "is born of love, and the moment one doesn't have love enough for the world, or love enough for language, or love enough for others—at that point one is dead as a poet."[5] In "My Surgeons" (1941) he has this as his credo: "Yes, I believe. In love." In an interview in 1972 he added a gloss: "I've always been an optimist about love. Three marriages are the proof."[6] Though the second part of this comment is possibly an ironic nonsequitur, it does serve as biographical support for the three unnamed feminine personalities who appear here and there in Kunitz's poems.

The most perceptive of Kunitz's critics, Jean Hagstrum, found *two* women in the poems:

. . . an Early Lady and a Later Lady. The Early Lady is imprecisely outlined. She appears fleetingly in the surrealist landscape of the first poems; and the experiences in which she figures are frustrating ones. . . .[7]

"A daughter of the sun" this "dear she" is "a strange wise child," "a fay"; hers is a "baby-heart"; she is compared to a bird, a leopard, a doe. (All of these quotations are from Kunitz's early poems.) This "she" figures in such poems in *Intellectual Things* as, among others, "A Daughter of the Sun," "Promise Me," "Strange Calendar," "Postscript," "Thumb-Nail Biography," "Regard of Tangents," and "For Proserpine."

Hagstrum suggests that "the situation" between this Early Lady and the "I" is one "in which one lover's love is too early and the other's is tragically late"[8] and quotes from "Regard of Tangents" in support of this:

> For love is coming or is passing by,
> And none may look upon her features plain.
>
> How shall these tarry, how shall these meet,
> When he must remember and she forget?
> Her baby-heart is running down a street
> Already ended, his to a place not yet.   (IT, 32)

So it may be, as Hagstrum has said, and yet the lines can be read, too, as pointing to an incompatibility of temperaments as specified in lines 2 and 3 of that poem: "Lean hip and deep familiar breast/Encounter opposites." It is at any rate in some way a fated, doomed love, and in the poem with the title "Promise Me," ironically playing on the title of the song so often sung at weddings, "O Promise Me," the poet addresses this woman as "dear she," and asks her to

> Think somewhat gently of, between
> Love ended and beginning, me.   (IT, 10)

In the poem that follows "Promise Me" in *Intellectual Things*, "Strange Calendar," the speaker himself promises his "Early One" a kind of enduring devotion:

> Yet one of me, arrived, shall pace the square;
> And one of me shall watch your not mine bed,
> Breathing upon your sleep; another shall have laid
> Himself in the revolving rock and, ageless, wait you there.
>   (IT, 11)

Hagstrum identifies this "Early One" with the "Dark Lady who spoke the serpent's word" of "The Dark and the Fair." Consequently, "the Later Lady . . . a person of wild adventuring spirit," in Hagstrum's words,[9] would have to be "the Fair" one of that poem.

Yet, between the two, the Early and Later Ladies, I think one can discern a shadowy figure of still another Lady, a Middle Lady, who seems to be the Dark one. This shade can be, certainly, a later version of the Early Lady, only that Early Lady seems too childlike and light-hearted to teach the "lesson" of that poem, what Hagstrum calls "a hard, hard lesson." This Middle Lady, then, if she be the Dark of "The Dark and the Fair," is a "handsome," "furied woman [who] did me grievous wrong. . . ." For her the poet "killed the propitiatory bird . . . ," and at the end of the poem he wishes "Peace to her bitter bones,/Who taught me the serpent's word, but yet the word" (SP, 34[10]). The imagery in this poem deliberately alludes to the Garden of Eden, and Kunitz himself has explicitly identified the Dark Lady as Lilith,[11] in medieval Jewish folklore the demonic first wife of Adam, hardly an apt characterization of the Early Lady described above.

Probably it is Lilith, this Dark, Middle Lady, who fails to telephone him in "No Word," is a shadow in "The Last Question," and also appears in other poems and in "Lovers Relentlessly" and in "Foreign Affairs." She it is, I think, who "Burned wanton once again/Through centuries of rain,/Smiling, as she must do,/To keep her legend true,/And struck the mortal blow . . . ," a Clytemnestra figure, in "A Spark of Laurel."

Hagstrum is surely right, though, in saying that the "Later Lady," the third Beloved Woman, "has provided both lover and artist with his deepest fulfillments . . . [and] has also evoked the most delicate, urbane, and courtly poetry Kunitz has as yet written." [12] She, the truly beloved, is the "dear girl" of "My Surgeons," the "dear" of "Night Letter," the "careless sprawler" and "Dreamer" of "The Science of the Night," and shows up also in a number of other tender love poems.

The point of all this is, I should say here, not which Lady is in which poem but that each of the three has "work to do," and categorizing these three faces or phases of Eve and Lilith here prepares us for the variety Kunitz brings to this single subject in his poems.

II *The Lost Father*

Another recurring person in Kunitz's poetry, the Father, is somewhat simpler to define than the Beloved Woman. Yet he, as well, has more than one face. "Two of Kunitz's best poems, 'For the Word is Flesh' . . . and 'Father and Son,'" Hagstrum writes, ". . . represent strongly diverse responses to antithetical father-images, or . . . antithetical responses to the same father-image, or perhaps something more complicated than either of these alternatives." [13] Kunitz's own father, Solomon Kunitz, a dress manufacturer, killed himself before the son's birth, and about him the poet has said that he knows "practically nothing aside from his name." [14] The father Kunitz did know was Mark Dine, his stepfather from his eighth to fourteenth years. He, too, died, "a gentle and scholarly man . . . who showed me," Kunitz writes, "the ways of tenderness and affection. His death . . . left me desolate." [15]

The significant facts about both of Kunitz's "fathers" are their loss and lack of presence for Kunitz man and poet; as a result Kunitz's real life mirrors the archetypal fable of the need to seek a lost father. Assuredly Kunitz's father-poems are among his best. One of those that Hagstrum cites in the quotation above, "Father and Son" from *Passport to the War* (1944) is a superb poem. "The Guilty Man" from that volume and "The Portrait" from *The Testing-Tree* (1971) are two other excellent father-poems. "For the Word Is Flesh" in

Intellectual Things (1930), which Hagstrum also praises as a superior
father-poem, while good enough, does not seem to me one of Kunitz's
"best" poems by any means.
   Besides references in these poems, the words "father" or "father's"
appear importantly in several others. In one the poet says that he will
go "till shadowless/With inner light I wear my father's face." In
another, "Father" is seen "prowling in a field/With speckled tongue
and a collar of flame." In others, "poor father's ghost [is] returned to
howl/His wrongs"; the poet himself clings "in hiding/To my father's
rotten wall"; also he cries "his father's grief . . ." and pretends "in a
childish voice/my father is not home."[16]
   In each of these instances, "father" is an obsessive, ghostly image.
So is he in the 1930 poem "For the Word Is Flesh," the third poem in
Kunitz's first book. The poem begins with an invocation to the father
harsh in tone and consistent with what follows: "O ruined father
dead, long sweetly rotten. . . ." The scene would appear to be the
cemetery in which lies Solomon Kunitz, his own father, whose suicide
followed the "ruining" of his business by a dishonest partner. The son
warns him here to "Beware a second perishing," that of being
"forgotten," and addressing him sharply as "Senior" asks,

> What shall the quick commemorate, what deeds
> Ephemeral, what dazzling words that flare
> Like rockets from the mouth to burst in air?   (SP, 44)

In the next stanza the separation between the son "quick" and the
"father dead" is widened by what seem intellectually arrogant
references to Lessius's "twenty-two/Fine arguments" and Tolet's
"sixty reasons/Why souls survive." He asks what the arguments and
reasons of these Jesuit writers on immortality are to his father and
what to himself, "who cannot blur/The crystal brain with fantasies of
Er. . . ." This allusion to Er, the protagonist in Plato's symbolic story
of the soul's journey to the next world, like the citings of Lessius and
Tolet, shows the poet wrestling with the whole problem of immortality.[17]
   While documenting Kunitz's handling of the lost-father theme, this
poem reveals its complexities, too, since "father" here is apparently
heritage as well as parent. Kunitz's attitude, as we shall see, toward
his Russian-Jewish ancestry changed through the years. Here
Christianity seems to be his preference; he hears "the fierce/Wild cry
of Jesus on the holy tree. . . ."

In contrast, of his father and his father's heritage he says he has "no syllable to keep,/ Only the deep rock crumbling in the deep." The poem ends with one of Kunitz's crisp, enigmatic epigrams:

> Let sons learn from their lipless fathers how
> Man enters hell without a golden bough.

The poem is denser and more allusive than most of Kunitz's other poems, which generally do not display esoteric learning. While the meaning may become clear some of the details in the poem are not. The words of the title, for instance, are central in the Christian doctrine of the Incarnation in which Christ is Logos, the Word. The relevant texts are John 1:1 and 1:14:

In the beginning was the Word, and the Word was with God, and the Word was God.
. . . .
And the Word was made Flesh, and dwelt among us; and we saw his glory, the glory as it were of the only-begotten of the Father, full of grace and truth.

The "For" of Kunitz's title makes the doctrine of the Incarnation in effect a conclusion—"for" meaning "because of, as a result of." The "is" puts it in the present as true now. In the poem "factual" in the "factual spikes" that "pierce/ The supplicating palms" of Jesus is linked by alliteration to and contrasted in meaning with the "fantasies of Er," the one Christian, the other Platonic. "Word," "words," and "syllable" lead toward the brief analogical narrative of the final stanza:

> Observe the wisdom of the Florentine
> Who, feeling death upon him, scribbled fast
> To make revision of a deathbed scene,
> Gloating that he was accurate at last.

What the Florentine[18] "scribbled" was words; the father, leaving his son "no syllable," contrariwise, leaves no legacy of words. Thus the son inherits no "golden bough" to guide him, and the father is "lipless," silent. The father in Kunitz's great father-poem, "Father and Son," ends similarly silent, turning to the son "The white ignorant hollow of his face." The feelings toward the fathers differ in the two poems; in this detail, however, they are implacably alike.

This later poem of Kunitz's, "Father and Son," the most written about of his works, is a piece of primordial power. Some of its effect surely comes from the universality of its dream-narrative based as it is on the aching, unassuageable grief a person can feel at the loss of a father, the sense that could one but find him again he would be able to answer all one's questions, solve all one's problems.

Overtly, then, "Father and Son" is in the tradition of the quest of the lost father, the son journeying in this poem down a "sandy road," through "fields," "years," following his father to "tell him my fable," the whole sequence of his life since his father's departure. He overtakes his father at last "At the water's edge, where the smothering ferns lifted/Their arms . . . ," symbolically at the last possible moment before his father's disappearance. "Father!" the son cries,

> "Return! You know
> The way. I'll wipe the mudstains from your clothes;
> No trace, I promise, will remain. Instruct
> Your son, whirling between two wars,
> In the Gemara of your gentleness,
> For I would be a child to those who mourn
> And brother to the foundlings of the field
> And friend of innocence and all bright eyes.
> O teach me how to work and keep me kind."   (SP, 45–46)

The son's narrative of the years since his father's death, and this—his cry, his promises, and his final request—just quoted, take up most of two narrative-blocks of the poem, seventeen of the thirty-four lines. The father, on the contrary, says nothing, and even his face at the end is a mere "white ignorant hollow": "ignorant," it has no knowledge to impart, did it speak.

The mainly loose blank verse lines of the four sections of "Father and Son" have an assertive authority and inevitability that the thirty rhymed lines of "For the Word Is Flesh" do not. Some of the difference surely is due to the years between the writing of the two poems: "Father and Son" is a 1940s poem; the other is from the late 1920s. The imagery is stronger and more memorable in the later poem—"whose indomitable love/Kept me in chains"; "The night nailed like an orange to my brow"; "whirling between two wars."

Still, it is not unfair to compare the two poems, for, as Jean Hagstrum points out, they "are obviously now intended to be read together since they are printed on opposite pages in the 1958 volume."[19] Both, too, are in the section of *Selected Poems* entitled

"The Terrible Threshold" containing such apocalyptic, semireligious poems as "Open the Gates," "Single Vision," "The Words of the Preacher," "He," and, perhaps, especially "Goose Pond," in which the protagonist again journeys through years "Until . . ./ He meets his childhood beating back/ To find what furies made him man" (SP, 56).

The title of this section of *Selected Poems*, "The Terrible Threshold," comes from the first poem, "Open the Gates," another strange dream narrative in which

> Here at the monumental door,
> Carved with the curious legend of my youth,
> I brandish the great bone of my death,
> Beat once therewith and beat no more.

When the "hinges groan,"

> I stand on the terrible threshold, and I see
> The end and the beginning in each other's arms.   (SP, 41)

The search for the father and for one's beginning or past are parts of a single unity, and, too, the father figure is inextricably bound up with that of his son or the Self, the other principal person in Kunitz's poems.

III   *The Self*

Since the majority of Kunitz's poems, subjective as they are, concern the Self or Man, as he is sometimes designated, here I shall simply outline the characteristics of this Self and postpone fuller analysis of his mutations until I discuss individual poems. Jean Hagstrum gives an excellent, concise explanation of "Kunitz's surrealist landscape":

Man dissolves in a cooking vat of chemicals that stands alone on a crumbling rock. A poetic speaker compares himself to a crystal bead in a crystal ball, "So pure that only Nothing could be less." Twilight invades a room in which glowing lions congregate and in which the poet, also tawny, awaits the approach of night, as the day and his heart spill their blood to slake his lips, when suddenly the moon, tawny like man and lion, materializes at the door. A human body swells in corruption until in death it becomes a whale that, like a derelict vessel, is pillaged by the curious. Lovers eat their ecstatic hearts and kiss in "complicate analysis of passionate destruction." The poet creeps deep into his own self, where he lies on the burning plumage of an angel and so lives his entire life at once.[20]

These curious details are from half a dozen different poems, a mere six from among the many which in like fashion diagnose the human condition. All six of these poems that Hagstrum quotes from appeared originally in Kunitz's first volume, *Intellectual Things* (1930). From that same book might be added these other strange, surrealistic activities: "your strange brain blooming," "A guilt not mentioned in our prayers, a sin/Conceived against the self," and "in my sleep/The ape, the serpent, and the fox I find/Shut with my soul in fortune's writhing sack."[21]

And so early, in his first book, Kunitz mapped his territory, and what subsequent poems and volumes do is fill in the flora and fauna of his vision of man and life, his "fable." It is a strange, terror-ridden world beset by "enemies of life," specific groups stigmatized as sadistic "surgeons," "bully-boys," "butcher-boys," and by guilt and chance and circumstance too.[22] The Self worries about the passage of time, and "identifies," it might be said, with the world's victims. In "The Man Upstairs," for example, a 1954 poem, the pathetic "gray somnambulist," the man upstairs, dreams "my future as his past." From suffering and "passion" (in its meaning of "agony") he "turns": "I turn; I perish into work." The fourth and final stanza of that poem immediately following these words, in its invocation, imagery, and detail, sums up this aspect of Kunitz's thought:

> O Magus with the leathern hand,
> The wasted heart, the trailing star,
> Time is your madness, which I share,
> Blowing next winter into mind . . .
> And love herself not there, not there.
>
> (SP, 30; ellipsis in text)

Mostly, though, the terrorized Self, an idealist, has found that the world and himself insufficiently measure up to his demands. He is "sick of crimes/Against us"; bitterly he hates "the good-enough that spoils the world"; and in his "prime, disburdened of my gear," he says that his "trophies [are] ransomed, broken, lost. . . ."[23] A part of himself is "Rover," his "no-name" and "nothing-knows,/Original

with fire and sin . . ." (SP, 85). Sometimes this part of himself or his
second self is "Heart," to whom he says,

> "Endure the lie,
> The waste, the tedium."
>
> My heart sank to his knees,
> Schooled in the tragic style,
> But I, being out of heart,
> Whipped him another mile. . . .   (SP, 76)

Continuing this doubleness, "The thing that eats the heart is mostly
heart" (SP, 71), and buying a mask from the "Prince of Counterfeits,"
the devil himself, the speaker declares it "the Self I hunted and knifed
in dreams!" (SP, 83). "Between the Acts," in its single quatrain, gives
this "drama in a nutshell" (SP, 114):

> Fate hired me once to play a villain's part.
> I did it badly, wasting valued blood;
> Now when the call is given to the good,
> It is that knave who answers in my heart.   (SP, 77)

This tone in Kunitz's poetry is what M. L. Rosenthal calls "the heavy
Baudelairean sense of secular damnation. . . ."[24] To Kunitz, as to
many modern poets, Baudelaire was "important,"[25] and it is not
surprising that he includes his translation of Baudelaire's "Au
Lecteur" in *Selected Poems*, the only translation in that volume. That
poem most terribly limns the evil in every man's heart: "Each day we
take another step to hell . . ." (SP, 89).

To this Kunitz adds an American dogged determination not to be
done in by guilt and horrors. In response to the "Wrath [which] has
come down from the hills to enlist/Me surely in his brindled
generation . . . ," he insists that he will "not warp my vision/To
square with odds; not scrape; not scamp my fiber . . ." (SP, 81). Still,
he is "The Guilty Man," and in the long (74 lines), important,
penultimate poem of *Selected Poems*, "Revolving Meditation," he
surveys his situation and asks the central question as to why he reacts
to life as he does:

> God knows I've had my joys,
> Tasted the honey on the branch
> And picked a sprig or two
> Of accidental laurel
> Along the way;

But why do I wake at the sound,
In the middle of the night,
Of the tread of the Masked Man
Heavy on the stairs,
And from the street below
The lamentation of the wounded glove?

Following that long question, he emits a sound of disgust, "Agh!" and says,

I am sometimes weary
Of this everlasting search
For the drama in a nutshell,
The opera of the tragic sense,
Which I would gladly be rid of.
A shameless keyhole god
Keeps spying on my worst. . . .

Later, in line 38, he asks, "Why should I be bothered with it?"

Imagination makes,
Out of what stuff it can,
An action fit
For a more heroic stage
Than body ever walked on.

This world, then, is insufficient for the Self, and the next world—well,

If I must build a church,
Though I do not really want one,
Let it be in the wilderness
Out of nothing but nail-holes.

"I listen, I am always listening," he adds,

In fear that something might get by,
To the grammar of the public places,
But I fly towards Possibility,
In the extravagantly gay
Surprise of a journey,
Careless that I am bound
To the flaming wheel of my bones. . . .

The tone of this poem, of which I have quoted nearly one-half, is similar to that in "A Choice of Weapons," a poem which precedes "Revolving Meditation" in *Selected Poems* and is concerned, too, with the poet's response to the horrors of life as he sees it. In "A Choice of Weapons" a critic asks the poet "why a gang of personal devils/Need clank their jigging bones as public evils" in Kunitz's poetry (SP, 113). This vision of the enlarging of "personal devils" into "public evils" is precisely "The burden of the personal" that is prominently the subject of Kunitz's poems (SP, 27).

So, finally, to the question as to what the poet believes, the answer is that he values life, man, the Self, and, though he prays to God, he is merely tempted by Christianity and institutionalized religion, not committed to them. And possibly he has been less tempted as the years have gone by and he has become reconciled to his Jewish heritage. An interesting revision is that of the poem entitled "He," about Christ: in Kunitz's first two books the pronoun "He" is capitalized in each of its four appearances; in his third book, *Selected Poems*, it becomes "he," a de-divinizing of Christ (SP, 53). Kunitz's own words in an interview affirm his religious interests: the Christian myth is more important in his poems than other myths, he said, "Because it shakes me more. It is the supreme drama of guilt and redemption. I have no religion—perhaps that is why I think so much about God."[26] Still, his explicitly religious poems such as "He" are less successful than others of prayer or indignation such as "Vita Nuova," "Father and Son," "My Surgeons," "Night Letter," "Robin Redbreast," or the late sequence "Around Pastor Bonhoeffer," in which his voice is a tender, humanistically concerned, basically religious one. Yet, as Stanley Moss wrote in his review of *The Testing-Tree*, "Kunitz has given us some of the great religious poems of our century."[27] And that, as will be shown later in closer analyses of some of his poems, he surely has done.

IV   *Matter Pouring through Eternal Forms*

For Stanley Kunitz, "The poem is an essential moment in the making of [the] fable" of one's life. "It is not a self-indulgence," he wrote in 1942,

like scratching one's nose; or a sentiment, however pretty; or a speculation, be it ever so fanciful. Like Hopkins' bird of peace, a poem does not come to coo; it comes with work to do.[28]

Or, as he wrote in "A Choice of Weapons" (1956), "The triggered poem's no water-pistol toy,/But shoots its cause, and is a source of joy" (SP, 113). For him, his "motives bleed/Even while strolling in a formal garden [the poem]." Kunitz's own "gang of personal devils/ . . . clank their jigging bones . . ." mainly on an inward stage, an inner, dark, troubled arena of dream, nightmare, and parable, of, as Ralph J. Mills, Jr., has said, "apocalyptic terror, enigma, and nihilistic forces,"[29] all held in check and pressed back from chaos by line, rhythm, rhyme, and, usually, stanza.

How all this is done can best be illustrated by looking closely at specific poems, to begin with, an early poem, "Vita Nuova." Appearing in *Poetry* magazine the month of Kunitz's twenty-fourth birthday,[30] this poem was used to close both his first and second books of poetry. Such a featured position suggests its importance and compels the reader's attention. The title, too, is striking in Kunitz; it is one of only two titles in *Selected Poems* not in English. ("Sotto Voce," almost an English phrase, is the other non-English title.) It is a strikingly suitable title, also, for the English "New Life" cannot bring in as "Vita Nuova" does the memory of this earliest of Dante's writings with its reference to Dante's early life and his life made "new" by love.

A self-portrait, a summary, and a prayer, "Vita Nuova" is representative of many of Kunitz's mature poems. First of all, it is highly personal, though not "confessional"; one discerns almost no distinction between the poet and the "I" of the poem. Further, the content, theme, imagery, tone, and form of the poem are all characteristic of Kunitz's poetry through the greater part of his career, that is, say, through 1958, the year of the publication of his third book of poems, *Selected Poems*. ("Vita Nuova" appears in that volume, as well as in the first two books, the third poem in the important last section of the book.)

As to the first point, in most of his poems Kunitz seems to be speaking in something very like his own voice, unlike the preference of many poets of the first generation of the moderns for masks and personae. "Now one of the marks of the lyric poet," he has said, "is a compulsion to expose . . . to show his mask."[31] Kunitz's "I," then, is a traditionally lyric "I"; like those of many previous poets—Wordsworth's or Coleridge's, for example—Kunitz's "I" displays a good portion of the "real" Kunitz. Yet perhaps "portion" should be emphasized, for some aspects of the man Kunitz as well as the life of man in general are decidedly excluded from the poetry.

Remembering Paul Valéry's warning not to suppose that the man whom the poetry presents to us is the real man who wrote the poetry, we can note that some of the more routine, ordinary, trivial, sometimes sordid activities of everyday life and thought that some contemporary poets unhesitatingly include in their poems simply are not in Kunitz's. His poetry deals rather with moments of heightened sensitivity and awareness, of self-revelation. "Formal verse is a highly selective medium," he said, and added, "A high style wants to be fed exclusively on high sentiments." [32] Until the 1960s and 1970s most of Kunitz's poems were formal in versification and consequently lofty in theme.

In "Vita Nuova," for instance, the "I" announces a Dantean "new life" of single-minded concentration rather than dispersion. He vows to "peel" from his brain the "vision" of the many conflicting selves of his past and

> . . . go, unburdened, on the quiet lane
> Of my eternal kind, till shadowless
> With inner light I wear my father's face.   (SP, 109)

In the final stanza prayerfully he invokes the "Moon of the soul" to

> . . . accompany me now,
> Shine on the colosseums of my sense,
> Be in the tabernacles of my brow.
> My dark will make, reflecting from your stones,
> The single beam of all my life intense.

It is a fierce, gloomy poem of self-examination and revelation, typically introspective and hard on the self in its asserting of a determination to be dedicated to a singleness man rarely achieves.

At the same time the poem is dense with Kunitz's exact diction and consistent imagery—verbs like "abdicate," "gnawed," and "peel"; nouns like "apocalypse," "visor," "colosseums," and "tabernacles" concisely pointing to the various traditions, Christian, medieval, Roman, and Hebrew. The only revisions in the poem between its first version and its last are minor. In line 7 "Cherishing beauty with the breath I keep" becomes "Cherishing life, the only fire to keep" in *Passport to the War*, and line 19, "My dark will make, reflecting thee at once" becomes "My dark will make, reflecting from your stones. . . ."

Both of these changes are mainly word substitutions, four words and five syllables for four words and five syllables in line 7 and three words, three syllables for three words, three syllables in line 19. They would seem to be made for sense, then, not meter or sound: the one revision enlarges from "beauty" to "life" and introduces the fire image; the other eliminates the sole archaism in the poem, "thee," and makes the moon image more concrete with "stones." This meagerness of alteration between one appearance of a poem and another is the rule with Kunitz; upon publication a poem is finished and seldom changed much subsequently.

"Vita Nuova," like most of Kunitz's poems until the late 1950s, is careful in form, four stanzas of five lines each, rhyming ababb. In each stanza the second b is a consonantal rhyme, not an exact one as are the others, giving somewhat the effect of ab^{1}ab^{2}b^1: "sup" and "up" in lines 2 and 5 but "lip" in line 4; "sense" and "intense" in 17 and 20 but "stones" in 19. This use of consonance in the fourth line of each stanza makes the music of the rhyme subtle and less insistent than it would be with three exact rhymes. At the same time rhyming different parts of speech—verb and noun, for instance, in the a rhyme and verb, noun, and preposition in the b rhyme of the first stanza—gives an additional richness to the rhyme. Then, too, in the ten-syllabled line of the poem Kunitz varies the caesura and skillfully replaces initial iambs with trochees ("Giving," line 6; "Moon of," line 16; and "Shine on," line 17).

Finally, the five-lined stanza of "Vita Nuova" closely resembles what might be called Kunitz's "favorite" or "favored" stanza, a quatrain rhyming abab with lines six to eight, and, sometimes, ten syllables long. More of Kunitz's poems are in quatrains than in any other form, nearly half of the total number of his poems. Yet having said that I have to note that the truly Kunitzian poem is rather one with long stanzas or verse paragraphs of a loosened blank or free verse—poems like "The Science of the Night" (stanzas of 11, 11, 9, and 13 lines), "Father and Son" (12, 10, 10, 2), "Foreign Affairs" (19, 10, 18), or "The Thief" (25, 21, 11, 16). These meditative poems, all in *Selected Poems,* are from thirty to eighty lines long. Some few poems in *The Testing-Tree*—"Journal for My Daughter" and "King of the River" are examples—are of this kind also, freer in verse but similar in strategy to the earlier reflective pieces just named.

These typically Kunitzian poems resemble Coleridge's "conversation poems" such as "Frost at Midnight" and "The Nightingale," and like them most usually they have specific settings and begin with a circumstance, a thought, an occasion, and go on to parse the reflection it sparks before resolving in an incandescent conclusion.

"The Science of the Night," a 1953 poem, is an example: forty-four lines of loosened blank verse divided into four sections of 11, 11, 9, and 13 lines, miserly in rhyme, this poem begins with the poet awake in the night beside a sleeping beloved. Asleep she has left him, he says, to go "Down the imploring roads I cannot take/Into the arms of ghosts I never knew," her own dream world, which he pictures as the infinity of space:

> I see the lines of your spectrum shifting red,
> The universe expanding, thinning out,
> Our worlds flying, oh flying, fast apart.   (SP, 3)

He recognizes how separate and apart they are as individuals, as persons, despite their physical closeness:

> We are not souls but systems, and we move
> In clouds of our unknowing
>   like great nebulae.
> Our very motives swirl and have their start
> With father lion and with mother crab.

These astrological signs of lion and crab, Leo and Cancer, marking the months of their separate births, stand for their differentness from one another.

In the fourth and final section of the poem he summons his beloved back, orders her, "Awake!"

> My whirling hands stay at the noon,
> Each cell within my body holds a heart
> And all my hearts in unison strike twelve.

The daylight world, "the noon," the *known*, is opposed to midnight, the unknown; the "science" or knowledge of the night that the poem delivers to us revolves around these two twelves, noon and midnight, and the word "twelve" with which the poem ends. The form of the poem itself is made up of twelveness, pulling back from or exceeding or touching twelve, lines lengthening out from the base of ten syllables to twelve ("In clouds of our unknowing . . .") and 11, 11, 9, and 13-lined sections, each just avoiding twelveness.

A striking contrast in form is the poem at the opposite end of *Selected Poems* from "The Science of the Night"—"A Spark of Laurel." This 1957 poem at the end of the book is written in unusually short six-syllabled rhyming couplets, eighteen of them presented in a single block. The situation of the poem is that a poet tells the "I" how he has remembered some lines from one of Kunitz's poems of "twenty years and more" ago. When this poet recites them he conjures up for the "I" the "she" for whom they were written. Thence the "I" reflects on the origin of poetry and ends by defining it as "both fire and stone,/Mother and mistress, one" (SP, 116).

In the single verse paragraph of eighteen couplets, the turn, "Ha!" comes exactly in the middle. Threads of "greekness" ("Euripides," "mortal blow," "sirens," "Ulysses," "Agamemnon"); fire ("burned," "laurel-sparking," "fire"); and poetic terms are woven through these short lines so that the poem is compact with a rich mystery. "The transubstantial word" and "The spiral verb" would seem to be what all poems might aspire toward—"Of myth and water made/And incoherent blood. . . ." To have the laurel "sparking" knits in with the fire imagery when the spark is viewed as "a glowing bit of matter, especially one thrown off by a fire" (as it is in one definition); but "spark" also has the meaning of "a tiny beginning or vestige, as of life, interest, excitement. . . ." When "This man, this poet" intones Kunitz's lines, he "sparks" in this sense this particular poem, "A Spark of Laurel." This occasion also "sparks," that is, stirs up, activates, the old hurt so that "she, long since forgotten" strikes "the mortal blow" again. This time it is bloodless; ". . . not that blood could flow." Instead, art, as the second half of the poem, succeeding this line, analyzes.

Both this poem, the last in *Selected Poems*, and "The Science of the Night," the first, traverse the map of the body with Kunitz's consistent anatomical imagery and also use parental terms ("father" and "mother") to achieve unity. Both poems center on a beloved woman, differing manifestations of "she." In both, "she" has knowledge to give the protagonist. In "The Science of the Night" by "the virtue of [her] honeyed word" she will "Restore the liquid language of the moon"; in "A Spark of Laurel" because of her, he hears "The transubstantial word." The poems differ in content and form, and so, too, marked though they are with his special sign, do Kunitz's other poems.

CHAPTER 3

This Laurel-Sparking Rhyme

POETRY is the subject of the poem. . . ." This observation of
Wallace Stevens's quoted by Kunitz in a 1972 interview[1] implies
that the writing of a poem is itself a theory of poetry, and so we might
infer that a poet's poetics is everywhere in his poems. Yet still it is in
some poems more than in others, and especially it is in those poems
which are explicitly about poetry and art. Here, in order to single out
the main elements in Kunitz's poetics, I shall examine some of his
poet and poetry poems and generalize from them.

First are some practical and theoretical remarks about poetry from
Kunitz's prose and from interviews with him—how a poem comes
about, what a poem is, and what relation the poem has to the poet. He
"writes" his poems, Kunitz said, "by saying them. . . . If it doesn't
satisfy my ear then I know it's wrong." He keeps putting down the
words as he says them, but does not at this point "take very seriously
what I'm writing. I let it flow, so that a lot of language spills onto the
page, and I don't know whether it's good or bad." Then, after
beginning a poem this way "in longhand, I type what I have, because I
need to get a sense of its look on the page." Following that, "It's a
process of building up line after line, discarding the earlier versions
and starting again from scratch. Any one poem can involve up to 100
sheets of paper, because it always starts from the beginning and goes
as far as it can." In this way he keeps rewriting, he says, "through
countless changes, saying it, chanting it, until a music begins to fill
me. Once I hear the beat, I'm in clover."[2]

In telling the story of the writing of one of his poems, "End of
Summer,"[3] Kunitz comments that the poems that he is "most
committed to are those that I recall fighting for hardest, through the
anxious hours, until I managed to come out on the other side of
fatigue, where I could begin to breathe again, as though the air had
changed and I had found my second wind." "End of Summer" came
about in the 1950s, he says, one afternoon in late September when he

47

was chopping weeds in the field behind my house in Bucks County, Pennsylvania. Toward sunset I heard a commotion in the sky and looked up, startled to observe wedge after wedge of wild geese honking downriver, with their long necks pointing south. I watched until the sun sank and the air turned chill. Then I put away my garden tools and walked back to the house, shivering with a curious premonition.

Later he worked in his study "until dawn to get the words down on paper. Nothing came that seemed right to me. Five days later I had hundreds of lines, but they still added up to nothing." Then,

In the middle of the fifth night I experienced a revelation: what was wrong with my enterprise was that I was attempting to compose a descriptive piece about the migration of the birds, whereas it was the disturbance of the heart that really concerned me and that insisted on a language. At this point I opened the window, as it were, and let the geese fly out. Then the poem came with a rush.

The five days of work resulted in a poem of sixteen lines, quatrains rhyming mostly abab; a few word substitutions—"An" and "A" at the beginnings of lines 1 and 2 for the original "The's," which had "made too thick a sound"; "amazed" for "surprised," "lisped" for "sang"— and the experience that had "insisted on a language" had one.

For that, in Kunitz's definition, is what poetry is—"language surprised in the act of changing into meaning." [4] In this definition he was, Kunitz has said,

differentiating . . . between the language of statement, of fact, and that language which is largely unconscious, which is drawn from the unconscious itself, and which therefore is not yet in the form of explication—and *should* not be, in terms of my concept of the poem. [5]

The common element in both Kunitz's own practice and in his theory is "language." Poetry resides in the words themselves, and thus for Kunitz the "word," the poem, is "transubstantial," "is flesh," truly creation, like God's creation of man, of Himself as the second person of the Trinity, a creation of independent, autonomous objects. To a group of students Kunitz said once that a certain poem of his own was "a long way" from himself by then and he was "glad" that he could not remember what he "had in mind." For what was in the poem, he continued, there were not any "right answers."

My intentions, even if I could remember them, are irrelevant; and my afterthoughts are not necessarily to be trusted. What matters—I say this hopefully—is the poem itself, in the give-and-take of each new encounter, as it struggles to come alive in your consciousness.

The mistake readers stumble into, what W. K. Wimsatt and Monroe Beardsley have called the "intentional fallacy," is in relying on the poet for the "right answers." The error here, Kunitz said, is "in supposing that the poem began as an idea, which was then transposed into verse. If that were true, we might as well publish the original idea and dispense with the poem that paraphrases it." On the contrary, Kunitz insists, "Usually the poet doesn't really have what could be defined as an explicit intention. The poem demands to be written and gives no peace until it's done."[6] This demand of the poem to be written, he wrote in *A Kind of Order*, "is a kind of prehensile thing. You don't know why you're writing poems, any more than a cat knows why it claws at the bark of a tree."[7]

This poem that "demands to be written" is the "overplus" of the self, to use the rather unlovely word for it in "Hermetic Poem," one of Kunitz's important poems about poetry. The word "hermetic" in that title derives from Hermes Trismegistus, the Greek name for the Egyptian god Thoth, the mythological founder of alchemy and other occult sciences, and in itself "hermetic" means magical and so points to this as a main characteristic of poetry, its inexplicable, mythic, unwilled quality. "Hermetic Poem" itself in ten short lines gives the violence and effect of poetry. "The secret my heart keeps / Flows into cracked cups," the poem begins. As in the prose description of the poetic process above, what the poet has to say "flows" and "spills," has a movement of its own:

> No saucer can contain
> This overplus of mine:
>
> It glisters to the floor,
> Lashing like lizard fire
>
> And ramps upon the walls
> Crazy with ruby ills.
>
> Who enters by my door
> Is drowned, burned, stung, and starred. (SP, 86)

Similarly in "The Illusionist" (SP, 78) the title figure is the poet who crisply in twenty-four short lines metaphorically lists his activities, which include playing "furious, grim charades" and parodying his life. Then in "Ambergris" what the artist provides is presented both as "ambergris" itself, the substance from the intestinal tracts of sperm whales used in perfumes, and as a kind of Holy Communion:

> Come pluck the deep wild kernel of my breast,
> That wafer of devotion, and partake
> Of its compacted sweetness. . . .   (SP, 74)

In conclusion he says that his "enemies will flee,/Whereas my friends will stay and pillage me." Like "the whale of death" of that poem, in "'What Have You Done?'" "pride, sores, excretion,/Blaz[e] . . . with death" and from the poet's

> . . . angry side
> Tumbles this agate heart,
> Your prize, veined with the root
> Of guilty life,
> From which flow love and art.   (SP, 87)

The final section of *Selected Poems*, "The Coat without a Seam," brings together eight of Kunitz's important poet and poetry poems. "Invocation" begins the section, and "A Choice of Weapons," "Revolving Meditation," and "A Spark of Laurel" successively end it. Published in 1930 in the *Nation*, the first of these four poems is made more mysterious by the abbreviating of its title in *Passport to the War* from "Invocation to the Phoenix" to, simply, "Invocation."[8] It is also somewhat revised and shortened from its magazine publication; these changes probably delayed its publication in book form until 1944, for poems published later in 1930 than this one were included in the 1930 volume *Intellectual Things*. "Invocation," itself, finally, in its finished form combines the legends of Prometheus and the phoenix to reach the conclusion that the poet (the Promethean figure) has defended "one incendiary vein"

> . . . to slake
> You in the burning, whose daemonic beak
> The clasp of bone about my heart O break!

Before considering the other three "poet and poetry" poems named above, all written in the 1950s, we should look at one other 1930s "poetry" poem, "Skull of Ecstasy," which did not appear in its ultimate form until 1958 in *Selected Poems*. In the *Nation*, under the title "Skull of Ecstasy," the poem had these three stanzas:

> Five dewy russets and a hill's sweet curve
> Burst in his forehead with a rainbow-spray
> Of atoms; tender phantoms of the nerve
> Melted in unrevolving light one day.
>
> Now that his heart is quiet, let him climb
> Over and under the mind; catch in his skein
> The shapes of things interior to time,
> Hewn out of chaos when the Pure was plain.
>
> Used bees with golden bellies ripped, be still.
> The bitter spider ravels out his wit
> Deep in the grated dungeon of the eye
> Where the old gods shaggy with gray lichen sit
> Like fragments of the antique masonry
> Of heaven: snared by five russets and a hill.[9]

In revision all but five of the original fourteen lines were discarded; these five were rearranged. The "Five dewy russets" (winter apples) and the hill, which began and ended the poem, the bees, the spider, and the rhyme were eliminated. The third person ("his") became first ("my"). The original sonnetlike poem became the following twelve-lined poem entitled "Among the Gods," setting forth a whole poetics:

> Within the grated dungeon of the eye
> The old gods, shaggy with gray lichen, sit
> Like fragments of the antique masonry
> Of heaven, a patient thunder in their stare.
>
> Huge blocks of language, all my quarried love,
> They justify, and not in random poems,
> But shapes of things interior to Time,
> Hewn out of chaos when the Pure was plain.
>
> Sister, my bride, who were both cloud and bird
> When Zeus came down in a shower of sexual gold,
> Listen! we make a world! I hear the sound
> Of Matter pouring through eternal forms.   (SP, 7)

What can briefly be said about the content of this poem is that poems are compared to pieces of sculpture, like the great works of Michelangelo, for example, which were there in the "blocks" awaiting the artist who could release them. In the brilliant and allusive third stanza, poem and poet like Zeus and Danae "make a world," Matter achieving a "shape . . . interior to Time."

All three of the 1950s "poetry" poems are more relaxed and intimate in tone than those just discussed, without any underlying mythical structure. "A Choice of Weapons," for instance, in three stanzas of four, five, and four rhymed couplets each, has the poet-speaker first stating the problem:

> Reviewing me without undue elation
> A critic who has earned his reputation
> By being always Johnny-on-the-spot
> Where each contemporary starts to rot
> Conceded me integrity and style
> And stamina to walk a measured mile,
> But wondered why a gang of personal devils
> Need clank their jigging bones as public evils. . . .   (SP, 113)

In the second stanza the critic speaks:

> "Though poets seem to rail at bourgeois ills
> It is their lack of audience that kills.
> Their metaphysics but reflects a folly:
> 'Read me or I'll be damned and melancholy.'
> This poet suffers: that's his right, of course,
> But we don't have to watch him beat his horse."

In the third and final stanza the poet answers him with an extended metaphor for his poetics:

> Sir, if appreciation be my lack,
> You may appreciate me, front and back—
> I won't deny that vaguely vulgar need:
> But do not pity those whose motives bleed
> Even while strolling in a formal garden.
> Observe that tears are bullets when they harden;
> The triggered poem's no water-pistol toy,
> But shoots its cause, and is a source of joy.

In "Revolving Meditation" the poet soliloquizes on the same theme in seventy-four undivided, unrhymed lines and ends by saying that he "prefers"

> . . . to hear, as I
> Am forced to hear,
> The voice of the solitary
> Who makes others less alone,
> The dialogue of lovers,
> And the conversation of two worms
> In the beam of a house,
> Their mouths filled with sawdust.   (SP, 115)

Lastly, then, in "A Spark of Laurel" the poet's experience, in this instance that of an old painful love, is shown as provoking art, tears becoming "bullets when they harden"—the "transubstantial word" and "The spiral verb." The latter is "Of myth and water made/ And incoherent blood. . . ." What "sirens . . ./ Trilled to Ulysses lost" is

> This laurel-sparking rhyme
> That we repeat in time
> Until the fathers rest
> On the inhuman breast
> That is both fire and stone,
> Mother and mistress, one.   (SP, 116)

Throughout this poem the imagery is traditional—fire, light, stone, blood—as is the sequence itself: out of suffering and pain comes art. And it is not entirely willed; the poet is "*forced* to hear,/ The voice of the solitary . . ." (my italics). But the whole has a religious or at least a sacramental aspect, too. In place of the bread and wine of the Eucharist are "myth," "water," and "blood." Ultimately the practice of art is healing: In the light-hearted poem "The Thief," the speaker recognizes "the gods' capricious hand" in the picking of his pocket in Rome because then he writes "this poem for money, rage, and love" (SP, 37). The poet's "choice of weapons" in the battle of life is "The triggered poem" which is "no water-pistol toy,/ But shoots its cause, and is a source of joy."

Both man and poet are perhaps most explicitly defined in the thirty lines of "Single Vision," the poem which alludes to the Blake quotation which is the source of the title of Kunitz's first book, *Intellectual Things*: "For a Tear is an Intellectual thing. . . ." The title of this poem of Kunitz's, "single vision," is also from Blake, who prayed, "May God us keep/ From Single vision & Newtons sleep. . . ." Earlier in that same poem Blake had defined the "double vision" as that of the inward and outward eye in which one sees "outward a Sun; inward Los [God] in his might. . . ." [10]

Kunitz's "Single Vision," like Blake's much longer poem (88 lines), is in couplets, too, with some similarity of rhyme: Blake rhymes "given-heaven" twice; Kunitz, "shriven-heaven" once; and in both poems the rhymes are mostly exact and single-syllabled. In Kunitz's "Single Vision" sacramental and Christ images combine in what seems to be a resurrection narrative of defiance. The speaker says that he will "reject my inch of heaven" and rise "to disown/The good mortality I won" (SP, 42). To his "ghost" he yields his "halved conscience, brightly peeled" and will "Infect him, since we live but once,/With the unused evil in my bones." Then, in conclusion, he will

> . . . shed the tear of souls, the true
> Sweat, Blake's intellectual dew,
>
> Before I am resigned to slip
> A dusty finger on my lip.   (SP, 43)

As is usual in Kunitz's poems, here the whole drama is played out on the stage of the poet's own person—his eyes, self, blood, side, mind, heart, skin, bone, skeleton, marrow, brain, conscience, finger, lip. It is his "eyes" that he will "Cancel"; "Into my deepest self" that he will "sink"; and

> The banner of
> My blood, unfurled, will not be love,
>
> Only the pity and the pride
> Of it, pinned to my open side.

When he has "utterly refined/The composition of my mind" and "Shaped language of my marrow till/Its forms are instant to my will,"

> Suffered the leaf of my heart to fall
> Under the wind, and, stripping all
>
> The tender blanket from my bone,

—only then will he "Rise like a skeleton in the sun. . . ."

In their own way the thirty lines of "Single Vision" are a complete exposition of Kunitz's idea of the poet, Blakean in the series of sharp pictures (the unfurled banner, the risen skeleton, the dusty finger on the lip) and at the same time quite Kunitzian in its compassionate tone. For, while for Kunitz the artist is "eternally guilty," he is also the "invincibly friendly man"[11] who pities humanity and for it sheds "the tear of souls."

I *Diction*

Whereas expectedly one finds echoes of earlier lyric poets in Kunitz's poems—as noted earlier the English Metaphysicals such as Donne and Marvell; others such as Milton, Baudelaire, and Rimbaud; moderns, Hopkins, Yeats, and Eliot—the one pervasive early influence on Kunitz would seem to be William Blake. Jean Hagstrum points to four poems in *Intellectual Things*, "none of which Kunitz has chosen to reprint" as "vaguely Blakean and romantic. . . ." These four are "Death in Moonlight," "Sad Song," "Thou Unbelieving Heart," and "Elemental Metamorphosis," all of which, as Hagstrum says, "remain flat and smooth and imprecise, like the romantics at their least impressive."[12]

"Open the Gates" of *Passport to the War* Hagstrum also sees as like Blake and similarly in *Selected Poems* four other poems in which "the Blakean strain grows into something fresh and lovely." The important element of Blake in Kunitz's early poetry must surely be, however, what Hagstrum calls "the verbal-visual Blake of emblems. . . ."[13] For repeatedly in Kunitz's poetry one *sees*, often a concrete word accompanied by an abstract one—the carved "lintel of a year," the brandished "great bone of my death," "the spiders of my dust," "the darkening glass that traps your shames," or "absence" which "Hangs on my chimney like a wreath of cloud."[14] At other times, in like fashion, Kunitz writes "the unloved year/Would turn on its hinge," "narrow transom of your will," "this house/Exhales resentment of audacious hope," phrases in which the abstractness of "year," "will," and "resentment" are given concrete form with hinges, transoms, houses.[15] One of the most vivid of these constructions is that in "Night Letter," where the speaker thinks he hears "A piece of laughter break upon the stair/Like glass . . ." (SP, 101).

Like both Blake and Yeats, Kunitz exploits the power of simple, homely English monosyllables and interestingly plays them off against Latinate polysyllables as they do also. In "The Hemorrhage," for instance, the monosyllables are "dark" and "rose"—"Exhibitor of the dark/Abominable rose"; in other lines, "blood" and "face"—"incoherent blood," "ignorant hollow of his face."[16] In some constructions a quality is transferred to a noun from something associated with it. Yeats does this in such a phrase as "beauty's ignorant ear" of

"The Scholars," in which "ignorant" belongs less to "ear" than to the whole person. In "the bestial floor" of Yeats's "Magi," the floor of the stable at Bethlehem is not in itself "bestial" but rather one on which beasts tread. In the "sleepless candle" of Yeats's "Phases of the Moon" the sleeplessness of the one who uses the candle to see by is transferred to the candle. Examples from other poets might be added—Chaucer's "dredful fot" in *Legend of Good Women* (Thisbe), Eberhart's "angry stick" in "The Groundhog," Wilbur's "sodden floor" in "A Voice from under the Table"—and in like manner analyzed. The point here, though, is the function of this contiguity.

This kind of construction itself is not, I think, the trope personification or prosopopoeia, either (investing abstractions or inanimate objects with human qualities or abilities). Even less is it Ruskin's "pathetic fallacy." Rather it seems to be a kind of catachresis, an effective collapsing of which poets have always availed themselves in order to make more condensed what they have to say.

"In all ages of poetry the fusion of the concrete and the abstract, the spatial and the conceptual aspects of *dianoia*," Northrop Frye said in *Anatomy of Criticism*, "has been a central feature of poetic imagery in every genre. . . ." [17] This particular figure, however, what Frye calls "'the adjective noun of noun' type, in which the first noun is usually concrete and the second abstract," Frye finds a favored twentieth-century variant of this ages-old device. In "examining a volume of twentieth-century lyrics I find," he wrote, "counting all variants, thirty-eight phrases of this type in the first five poems." "The pale dawn of longing," "the broken collar-bone of silence," "the massive eyelids of time," "the crimson tree of love" are examples that Frye made up himself and offered "free to any poet who wants them. . . ." [18]

Examples from Kunitz's poems are the "postman with the smiling hand," "The white ignorant hollow of his face," "her sleeping arm," and "I stood in the disenchanted field," in which the "hand" certainly is not "smiling" and the "hollow" itself is not "ignorant." In a sense the field *is* "disenchanted" because the beauty of summer is over, but even more the "I" of the poem is the disenchanted one. [19]

Another category of figures of speech in Kunitz's poetry—rather more prominent because of its flamboyant insouciance—is that of the "surreal," that is, an image that attempts to portray the material of dreams: "stretched into bird," "The silence unrolling," "The night nailed like an orange to my brow," and "I walk . . ./ through the deep litter of the years." The first three of these are from "Father and Son" (SP, 45), clearly a dream-narrative; the fourth is from "River Road"

(TT, 31), a rather more "realistic" poem. The difficulty some readers have found with these images is that they cannot "see," "imagine," or "believe in" them.[20] The difficulty is genuine. It is possible, I think, to explain the *feeling* or implication in each of these and even to *see* the first, "stretched into bird," if one imagines a surrealistic painting of a running or flying figure being transformed into a bird. Primarily, though, these are "natural and impossible" actions, as Robert Lowell says in commenting on "Father and Son"[21]—both "natural *and* impossible." It seems to me that, like the collapsed trope, they are not meant to be seen or imagined or believed in but felt or accepted: they appeal not to the "mind's eye," but instead to the "mind's mind," and Kunitz's own explanation of the most notorious of these, the "night-orange," can help: "Most of us must have known breathless nights, so heavy and close that the moon has walked with us. To suffer this night of the moon so intensely is to be impaled by it."[22] He further explains the "long history of association [of nail and fruit] in my mind" and adds that

the image . . . is an emanation of my felt truth. Such moments in a poem, evident only by the pressure building behind them, can never fully explain themselves, but the poet must take his risk with them as an article of faith. In the end, for whatever it may be worth, they constitute his signature.[23]

His signature, yes—both the collapsed image discussed above, "postman with the smiling hand" and this one, "The night nailed . . . ," are what we come to expect on occasion from Kunitz and to look forward to.

One biographical note on Stanley Kunitz points out: "Born . . . of Russian parents Kunitz applied himself to mastering the English language while still a child, and the acquisition of new words became his hobby."[24] The "acquisition of new words" or just *words* themselves no doubt *are* a hobby for most writers. W. H. Auden's parlor games with the OED are a well-known example of another poet's interest in words of all kinds. For himself, Kunitz said, words "always fascinated" him, even though he might not know what they meant. He cited as an example that in the fourth grade he "began a composition . . . with the sentence: 'George Washington was a tall, petite, handsome man.'"[25] The central question, nonetheless, as Kunitz phrased it in *A Kind of Order*, is "How to make words potent and magical again, how to restore their lost vitality?" For, as he said there, "One of the familiar grievances of the modern poet is that language gets more and more shabby and debased in everyday usage, until even the great words that men must live by lose their lustre."[26]

The infrequency of Kunitz's revisions and the variety of his diction suggest that before publishing a poem he attends to restoring the "lost vitality" of words with extraordinary care. If the finished poem on publication proved eventually to be unsatisfactory, Kunitz discarded it rather than work on it further. Thus fourteen years later the best poems from his first book, *Intellectual Things*, were placed virtually unchanged into the second section of *Passport to the War*, and some twenty-six poems, with only two exceptions, were, it seems, permanently jettisoned. In turn, the fifty poems of *Passport to the War* were included fourteen years later in *Selected Poems*, along with two poems, unchanged, resurrected from *Intellectual Things*.

But it is in the selection of the words themselves that a good part of Kunitz's power lies. While overall his diction is like Yeats's, chaste, decorous, and frequently polysyllabic, one notes no obvious imitation or mimicry—only an occasional echo, no more—and a healthy range like Yeats's between a colloquial turn or a lusty profanity and literary elegance. Hence Kunitz uses an unusual word like "lintel" in the same short poem as the homely expression "damn the cost." A good many of Kunitz's most memorable lines make similar combinations. In "A Choice of Weapons" the critic concedes him "Stamina to walk a measured mile," for instance: "Stamina" is a relatively formal word; "measured mile," while metaphorically it refers to poetic meter, is a phrase which appears on instructional roadside signs by which motorists are to check the accuracy of their speedometers.

Most often Kunitz adheres to the direct, straightforward subject-verb-object sequence: "A little wind investigates the page" (SP, 71), or,

> An agitation of the air,
> A perturbation of the light
> Admonished me the unloved year
> Would turn on its hinge that night.   (SP, 48)

Eighteen of the twenty-two words of this stanza are single-syllabled, but the force of the sentence is in the two four-syllabled noun-subjects, "agitation" and "perturbation," and in the three-syllabled verb "Admonished," the latter precisely in the middle of the stanza and the sentence (the eleventh word). Other strong, syntactically direct lines are these: "The dead would murder action," "a sulky weather dogs the heart," "My surgeons are a savage band," "I hate the good-enough that spoils the world," and "The years of my life were odd that now are even."[27]

Some of these quotations have a mnemonic epigrammatic quality, too, as do these: "principle disgraced, and art denied"; "Tempers could sharpen knives, and do . . ."; "doomsday is the eighth day of the week"; "We are what we are, and only life surprises"; "Redemption hangs upon the nails"; "with each elm a century went down."[28] No small art goes into such compression, for each word has to "count" if a universal truth of any sort is going to be stated in, say, as few as five words: "principle disgraced, and art denied."

Another characteristic of Kunitz's diction is his rare use of unusual words or words used in an unusual sense, often returning us to root meanings. "Ambages," "minatory," "peristyle," "polyp," "veridical," and "volute" are words which might need to be looked up, so out of the ordinary are they;[29] I find few other similarly "hard" words. For their own purposes poets traditionally have used words in a slightly off-center way: sometimes to get us to look at a word more closely, to think about its meanings, or simply to attract our attention. Most often, though, as in Kunitz, the strange word or the strange use of the word is meant to enlarge and enrich our vision of the world, to get us to think about it in its root sense: "language surprised in the act of changing into meaning."

So, when Kunitz writes "A little wind investigates the page," the four-syllabled "investigates" calls attention to itself in the mostly monosyllabic line and what visually would be a lifting and fluttering of the page becomes an inquiring into systematically, a checking and cross-checking of references (SP, 71). Something similar is true, too, when Kunitz writes that the critic may "appreciate" him, "front and back": while "appreciate," following upon "appreciation" in the previous line, can simply mean to think well of or esteem, its "appraise" meaning comes in with "front and back" so that, slyly, it is as though the poet were saying, yes, surely, the critic might well appraise him as though he were a prize horse (SP, 113).

Other strong and effective verbs are "dogs" in "a sulky weather dogs the heart" and "ramps" in "ramps upon the walls" in "Hermetic Poem" (SP, 86); or, "scamp" in "scamp my fiber" in "Welcome the Wrath" (SP, 81). An unusual noun is "get" in "Reflection by a Mailbox"—"the powerful get of a dying age . . ." (SP, 94). Here "get" is used in its "begotten" meaning, "progeny" or "offspring," a limited usage today. William Faulkner uses it to refer to animal, not human,

offspring, particularly those of horses, and Hugh Kenner applies to
the Minotaur the phrase "the unnatural get of a Cretan bull on Queen
Pasiphae. ..."[30] In Kunitz's line questioning the origin of "the
hunters of man-skins in the warrens of Europe" the noun "get" says
much about the nonhuman quality of "the hunters."

In the phrases "flagrant smile" and "my most flagrant source,"
"flagrant" may seem not quite to convey the usual dictionary sense,
though "glaringly bad," "notorious," and "outrageous" are meanings
consonant with these uses.[31] In "Hermetic Poem" "glisters" ("glisters
to the floor") may look at first like a misprint for "glistens," which it
closely resembles but differs from etymologically. "Glister" can be an
archaic variant for "glisten" but with the added "to" the verb acquires
movement as well as the appearance of static shining; it comes to rest,
finally, as it does in the dictionary, between "glisten" and "glitter"
with a meaning of its own (SP, 86).

As a concluding example of Kunitz's interest in acquiring "new
words," we can look at his use of "brindled" in "Welcome the Wrath"
(SP, 81). In this wartime poem, "Wrath" is specifically the war and
generally the evil of the world. Wrath comes

> ... down from the hills to enlist
> Me surely in his brindled generation,
> The race of the tiger; come down at last
> Has wrath to build a bonfire of my breast
> With one wet match and all man's desolation.

As with "get" above, "brindled" is ordinarily used to refer to animals
rather than to humans or human generations—as in "a brindled
cow." But its meaning of "having a gray or tawny coat streaked or
spotted with a darker color" is apt and meaningful here, pointing to
the moral ambiguity of the times.

II   Principal Categories of Words in Kunitz's Poetry

Of the major word-groups in Kunitz's poetry two are 1) metaphysical–religious words like "apocalypse," "tabernacle," "transubstantial," "sacramental," "pentecost," and 2) scientific words like
"corolla," "aurora," "nebulae," "spectrum" "ventricle." These two
kinds, though the least often used, loom prominently; the length and
uniqueness of these two kinds of words make them stand out. Still, a
close reading of Kunitz's poetry reveals that most of his other images,

comparisons, and citations come from three other major word-groups: 3) domestic objects and familial situations—"house," "door," "mirror," "mother," "father"; 4) the natural world of the heavens, insects, animals, birds, and vegetation; and 5) the world of the body in which, while "bone" and "heart" are the most repeated words, almost every area of the body from head to heel is touched on and named, as also are bodily aspects such as "smile," "kiss," "breath," "thought," and "dreams."

What this means is that, despite the learned and esoteric appearance of some of Kunitz's poems, at the center of his poetry is a core of everyday experience and reality. "Such mysteries for a Worcester childhood!" Kunitz exclaims in a final note to *The Testing-Tree*, after explaining the ruralness of his boyhood surroundings "at the thin edge of the city, with the woods beyond. Much of the time," he goes on, "I was alone, but I learned how not to be lonely, exploring the surrounding fields and the old Indian trails" (TT, 67). And so despite his birth and boyhood in Worcester, Massachusetts, one of the more industrialized, less attractive cities of New England, the poet is attached to the country, not the city. As an adult, too, he preferred "to be close to nature," as biographical sketches and Kunitz himself emphasized. And so he "spent much of his life in the Connecticut and Pennsylvania countryside," though he worked for a New York City publishing house. He managed this by editing the H. W. Wilson Company's massive reference works at home, going into New York at first every couple of weeks and then at longer and longer intervals. More recently he lived on Cape Cod for half of the year and in Greenwich Village in New York City for the remainder; in both places he had a garden, both unique, designed creations, the one in Provincetown a local showpiece. He "couldn't live in the city without a garden," he said; his "own favorite reading is in horticulture and zoology . . ." with "horticulture . . . a passion of" his. "Gardening," he said, "is a very deep, intimate part of my poetic life." [32]

The world of Kunitz's poetry, then, is a domestic and rural landscape of home and family, heaven, earth, sun, moon, stars, ponds, and roads (not city streets), rocks, stones, a treed, grassed, flowered, almost microscopic world in which one travels over the whole of the human body. A primary relationship is that of the father and after that, child and children, then the mother with brother, daughter, sister, and wife now and then. The house and its parts, doors, walls, halls, floors, windows, chambers, stairs, transoms, and lintels are mentioned and, as well, mirrors.

Referred to even more frequently are different items of the insect and animal world from creatures like worms, moths, beetles, flies, ants, bees, and others, to serpents, turtles, crabs, rats, moles, weasels, monkeys, cats, rabbits, dogs, and on to fox and ape, goat, leopard, doe, marmoset, whale, tiger, and lion. Birds figure most largely of all creatures with a couple of dozen references to them generically ("bird," "birds") and specific namings of robin, swallow, crow, dove, owl, swan, hawk, eagle, and buzzard.

In the vegetative world the parts of plants, especially those of flowers, are more frequently cited than those of trees, though trees are named also, noted as "tree" or "trees," "forest," "wood," "woods" with "limbs," "branches," "boughs," and "trunks." Of flowers, however, each part is named, and, as well, many individual plants: seed, root, leaf, stem, bud, bloom, petal; cinnamon-fern, water lily, marigold, violet, peony, rose, cucumber-vine, laurel, clover, cattail, Jack preacher, forsythia, hydrangea.

Besides the words "body" and "bodies" several times, nearly every part of the body would seem to be named in Kunitz's poems: cell, vein, artery, blood, bowel, lung, gut, marrow, heart, womb, pelvis, gristle, fat, heel, foot, leg, knee, shank, hip, hock, behind, breast, wrist, finger, thumb, arm, hand, ear, eye, lid, face, hair, head, and others. Of these "head" (along with "brain" and "thought" and "mind") and "hand" are frequent, with "bone," "eye," and "heart" being each successively more often used.

For Kunitz, as for poets traditionally and for both Blake and Yeats, "heart" is more than the muscle that maintains circulation and life. It is the person himself, his innermost self, his soul, "O Heart," with apostrophes to or personifications of heart, as in Yeats's poems "The Folly of Being Comforted" and "Owen Aherne and His Dancers." In a late poem Kunitz achieved a verbal irony by moving from "heart" in this larger sense—the whole person, his feelings—down to the specific physical organ: ". . . the hearts I spoiled, including at least/my own left ventricle . . ." (TT, 8). The word "heart" recurs more often than any other substantive in Kunitz's poetry. Along with "love('s)" and "honey," "rose," "moon," "soul," and "dreams" it contributes a note of romantic extravagance offset in individual poems, I think, by the specifics of less romantic words, "sockets," "bone-case," "teeth," "guts," "shanks," and "tongue."

Some kinds of words used by contemporary poets and acceptable in contemporary poetry simply do not appear in Kunitz's verse. For example in translating Baudelaire's "Au Lecteur" (which he says is

"For Stanley Kunitz") Robert Lowell uses such indelicate words as "whores," "pissing," "tits," "boozing," and "fuck." In Kunitz's earlier translation of the same poem only one of these words appears ("whore"), and while Lowell's gruesome creature of stanza 8 "suck/ snatch and scratch and defecate and fuck," Kunitz's "screech, howl, grovel, grunt. . . ." [33]

III The Intricacy of Kunitz's Diction

How Kunitz's diction works in his poems, though, is a subject to be taken up later. Here I simply want to suggest what his diction shows that his world is and is not: it would seem to be the classic landscape of small-town, even nineteenth-century, America, man close to nature—no city scenes, no cars, no streets, no hotels, no cafés, not even mountains or brooks or falls. Rather it is man in the world troubled by his actions and his emotions and their relationship to the universe.

The early sonnet "So Intricately Is This World Resolved" can be looked at as an example of the "intricacy" or elaborate interlocking of Kunitz's diction:

> So intricately is this world resolved
> Of substance arched on thrust of circumstance,
> The earth's organic meaning so involved
> That none may break the pattern of his dance;
> Lest, deviating, he confound the line
> Of reason with the destiny of race,
> And, altering the perilous design,
> Bring ruin like a rain on time and space.
>
> Lover, it is good to lie in the sweet grass
> With a dove-soft nimble girl. But O lover,
> Lift no destroying hand; let fortune pass
> Unchallenged, beauty sleep; dare not to cover
> Her mouth with kisses by the garden wall,
> Lest, cracking in bright air, a planet fall.   (SP, 58)

The theme of this poem is emphasized in the use of the first line as title; it is also how the poem itself is put together—"intricately . . . resolved" in music, for instance, and in the shifting of diction between the abstract and the concrete, drawing from almost every one of the categories listed above.

Kunitz's delicate music here is in the end rhyme, alternating except for the final couplet, and in the inner echoes such as "substance-circumstance" in line 2; "lest-line," line 5; "reason-race," line 6; "ruin-rain," line 8; "Love-lie," line 9. The metaphysical abstraction of the first seven lines of the octave with the Latinate and polysyllabic diction—"intricately," "resolved," "substance," "circumstance," "confound," "Perilous"—contrasts with the words in the eighth and succeeding lines, which, except for "destroying" and "Unchallenged," are one or two-syllabled with both lines 8 and 9 nearly a succession of monosyllables.

> Bring ruin like a rain on time and space.

> Lover, it is good to lie in the sweet grass. . . .

And then also "ruin" in its resemblance to "rain" hardly seems a two-syllabled word, though it is, and "Lover," at the beginning of line 9, balances "lover" at the end of line 10. With its insistence on the dangers of life and love and with the portentous "cracking" in the last line, the poem is typical of Kunitz in content, theme, and diction. From *Intellectual Things* (1930), it was reprinted unchanged in *Passport to the War* (1944) and then placed in the mathematical center of *Selected Poems* (1958). Like "Vita Nuova," the poem which concluded his first two books, "So Intricately Is This World Resolved" is a central poem in the Kunitz canon.

CHAPTER 4

The "Interior Logic" of Kunitz's First Three Books of Poetry

K UNITZ tends "to think," he said, "of a book as a composition, a joining of parts into an architectural whole, not just a throwing-together of the poems as written. A book ought to have an interior logic. . . ."[1] What is the "interior logic" of each of Kunitz's first three volumes? Both *Intellectual Things and Passport to the War* contained exactly fifty poems each, and each began and ended with significant poems. The first book began with "Change" and without internal divisions proceeded on to conclude with "Vita Nuova." The second book in turn began with a war poem congruent with its date of publication, "Reflection by a Mailbox," and finished off with the same poem as the first book, "Vita Nuova."

Part I of this second book *Passport to the War* contained twenty-six new poems, all those written since 1930 that Kunitz wished to retain; Part II, twenty-four poems from *Intellectual Things*. All fifty of these poems reappeared in *Selected Poems* with the addition of two poems from *Intellectual Things* which had not been carried over into *Passport to the War*. With that latter book already including poems from *Intellectual Things* and the poems from that book (*Passport*) all reprinted in *Selected Poems*, one gathers that *Selected Poems* is a collection of all the poems written up to that time that Kunitz wanted to keep, a kind of "collected poems" after all: more than half the poems from his first book and the whole of his second book. Yet, since Kunitz never arranged his poems chronologically, their juxtapositions in each book have significance, an "interior logic," as he phrased it; thus, next is an examination of this "interior logic" in each of his first three books along with a brief look at the poems rejected for one inadequacy or another.

I   Intellectual Things *(1930)*

First of all, as Kunitz reminds us, the poems in his first book, *Intellectual Things*, "date from 1927, when I was 22." He was, then, he says, "an innocent in so many ways. I had developed intellectually more than I had emotionally or experientially."[2] One can add "technically," too, for the failure of a good many of the poems in this book is due not to the inadequacy of theme or content but to questions of form and control. But first the book itself, its "interior logic": Lacking marked internal divisions and subtitles, the fifty poems rest rather heavily on the Blake epigraph "The tear is an intellectual thing." He "meant to demonstrate," Kunitz said, "if I could, not that the poem was a cerebral exercise, but the contrary, that the intellect and the passions were inseparable. . . ."[3]

This unity is, I think, the main emphasis in the volume, and the arrangement of the poems appears to be from generalities to particulars. Thus the first half of the book has poems which are relatively general visions of man, the poet, and destiny—poems like "Change," "Geometry of Moods," "Single Vision," "The Words of the Preacher," "Mens Creatrix," and "Ambergris." The second half has a good number of love poems, many of which were ultimately discarded. Seventeen of the twenty-six poems not reprinted in *Passport to the War* are from the second half of *Intellectual Things*. The earlier poems in this first book, the general ones, have overtones of doom, intimations of vision as, one can suppose, the poet grows. Finally, it seems that the poems attempt to reconcile or bring together "mind" and "heart," which along with "blood," "Time," and "thought," are among the most frequently used words in the book. Out of love and the suffering and pain it causes come poetry and the unity of the mind and the passions.

The book ends with some meditative-philosophical poems, "Who Tears the Serpent from the Flesh," "Organic Bloom," and, last of all, "Vita Nuova," presenting a hard, more terrifying vision of life—or of a "new life": the poet's dedication of himself to a more iron control. He had been "a part-time creature," and what he desires is "The single beam of all my life intense." This final assertion, the last line in *Intellectual Things*, confirms directly some of the incidental wisdom of other poems—in "The Words of the Preacher," for instance, "By piecemeal living a man is doomed . . . ," and in "Beyond Reason" he tames the passions "with the sections of my mind" and teaches his "mind to love its thoughtless crack."

II *Rejected Poems*

Of the two dozen or so poems from *Intellectual Things* which did not fit into the "interior logic" of *Passport to the War*, Kunitz has said that his own "main feeling" about them was "that they were immature. Maybe I felt a little embarrassed reading them, so I thought it would be better to drop them. . . ."[4] "Immature," yes, and sometimes embarrassing, too, but mostly they lack technical control, are awkward in imagery, and, at times, are awkward in form also.

The greater number of these rejected poems, more than one-half, can be grouped as "love" poems in which, often, "love is coming or is passing by" (IT, 32). "Thumb-Nail Biography" (IT, 27–28) shares weaknesses with many of the other poems in this grouping. It has an ugly title, for one thing, as do also "Particular Lullaby" and "Regard of Tangents" and other abandoned poems. Then in six short-lined quatrains with an abab rhyme the subject of a too-soon blossoming love is presented in rather infelicitous imagery ("delicate knobs of blooms," "electric light"):

> Her dim corolla-love,
> Believing there was sun,
> Received too early shivering proof
> Of corruption. (Stanza 4)

The last stanza wafts off helplessly in two sets of periods of ellipses as though the poem could not be brought to a conclusion.

Another love poem, "First Love" (IT, 47–48), too, fails in imagery, diction, and resolution. Here the Lady awakes to love so:

> At his incipient sun
> The ice of twenty winters broke,
> Crackling, in her eyes. (Stanza 1)

In the final, eighth stanza, she is said ineffectively to be,

> . . . a tree in spring
> Trembling with the hope of leaves,
> Of which the leaves are tongues.

"Me and the Rock" (IT, 42) also has a disagreeable title, and while its minimal punctuation gives it some interest as an early experimental poem, its untypical diction—"train," "cars," "planes," and "motors" —and unsuccessful images—"coals of remembrance," "blind/Punctures of sleep"—might be why it was not retained.

Two other eliminated poems, "Thou Unbelieving Heart" and "Sad Song" (IT, 43–44 and 45) might, it seems to me, be retitled, slightly revised, and revived. They are not highly significant, but both interestingly experiment with form, few rhymes, and a certain refrainlike quality. "Sad Song" is somewhat in "La Belle Dame sans Merci" tradition: "I married me a fay,/I was a merry gnome . . ." of stanza 1 becomes "I married me a fay,/I am a withered gnome . . ." of the third and final stanza.

In a four-stanza form (stanzas of 7, 8, 9, and 7 lines) reminiscent of the balade, "Thou Unbelieving Heart" with pseudomedieval matter ("lady," "lord," "hawk," "hound," "beast") tells a mysterious story the sinister implications of which are not clear. "Lady," the second stanza reads,

> . . . the bird still screams,
> The old dog licks his hand,
> Do not study your dreams.

The last stanza repeats the two opening lines of the poem:

> Lady that flutters in the bridal cage
> Waiting love's absent lord,

and then recasts the remaining five lines of stanza 1 using almost identical rhymes:

> The beast he hunts and may not find
> Is hunting you who shall be found.
> Erase the picture from your floor.
> Innocent Lady, you have heard
> The lion thunder at your door.

In contrast to these cast-off poems, the two poems resurrected from *Intellectual Things* for inclusion in *Selected Poems*, "Postscript" and "Benediction" (SP, 16–17 and 11–12), are more specific and more typical of Kunitz in both tone and idiom. The only changes in "Postscript" between its publication in 1930 and that in 1958, twenty-eight years later, are the excisings of the two archaic "unto's" in lines 3 and 39. The forty-three unrhymed lines of this single verse paragraph are, it seems, a "postscript" to a love affair. The speaker calls his dream journey of the first five lines "the perilous way without return," making it archetypal. He sums up what has happened in lines 14 and 15: "I lost by winning, and I shall not win/Again except by loss." Meanwhile he remembers and finds "Some little comfort" in thinking that "Yet will its lyric history be saved. . . ."

Yet, as the speaker says in the most memorable lines of the poem, art cannot feed man:

> A man can starve upon the golden-sweet
> Impossible apples of Cezanne; a man
> Can eagerly consult a woman's head
> (Picasso's), but her slow and stupid eyes
> Drink light in vegetative apathy.

With a final "O darling" cry he ends, rather weakly,

> The meaning of a mouth, a breast, is plain,
> But what you mean to me is dipped in blood
> And tangled like the bright threads of a dream.

What "a breast, a mouth" are in themselves "is plain," but what the poet means by their "meaning" is not. And "what you mean to me" in the next line is Valentine phrasing unredeemed by the strong phrase "dipped in blood" or the imprecise "tangled like the bright threads of a dream."

The other revived poem, "Benediction," in fifteen equal open couplets, is what its title says it is, a "benediction," a blessing, in which the speaker asks God first to

> . . . banish from your house
> The fly, the roach, the mouse . . .

and also to "Admonish from your door/The hypocrite and liar. . . ." Fear, doubt, evil are in turn to be excluded, as are surprise and delirium. In the last four couplets the speaker asks God to grant "you" tears, love, and his own "(My sweet) sweet company." It is a slight, uncomplicated occasional poem with no outstanding lines except for the wordplay on "sweet" in the final couplet, but overall a directness and competence that make it worth preserving.

III   Passport to the War *(1944)*

Arranged in two parts, part I new poems and part II poems
from *Intellectual Things, Passport to the War,* Kunitz's second
book, is in a sense his selected poems of 1944—and so it is subtitled:
"A Selection of Poems." The twenty-four reprinted poems, "some
of them revised," according to Kunitz's note, are grouped as
they were in the 1930 volume; the excisions make the progress
from "Change" to "Vita Nuova" clearer than it had been previously,
though part II reads rather like a separate volume than as a section intrinsically and necessarily following the twenty-six new poems
of part I.

These new poems, quite a bit more concrete, less abstract than
those in part II, are concerned with contemporary events seen as
timeless equivalents of the ills of the world. The time itself is that of
World War II, and the poems move from the poet's summons
to take part in the conflict ("Reflection by a Mailbox") through
further reflections on this and on the meaning of what is happening to him "whirling between two wars," who "Yesterday . . . had
a world to lose." Much of the imagery and many of the themes
of these poems relate to his enlisting in wrath's "brindled generation" and going "forth to war." About midway in the section
the poems seem to locate the source of the world's evil in man
himself, his "ancient wrongs," as in "Between the Acts," "The
Guilty Man," and "The Fitting of the Mask." It is his "wound,"
he says in the last poem of part I. The title of this poem, in quotation marks, poses a question asked of the poet, "'What Have
You Done?'" He answers it by asking his questioner, "Pigeon," a
loved one, to

> Be patient with my wound:
> Too long I lay
> In the folds of my preparation,
> Sinuous in the sun,
> A golden skin,
> All pride, sores, excretion,
> Blazing with death. O child,
> From my angry side
> Tumbles this agate heart,
> Your prize, veined with the root
> Of guilty life,
> From which flow love and art.   (SP, 87)

The title phrase, "'What Have You Done?'", is sufficiently everyday in diction to be a question actually asked of the "I" of the poem; still, the quotation marks make it seem more than that. Possibly it is an allusion to Pliny's "Hodie quid egisti?" so that while the question, first of all, asks about a specific act (such as going off to war) it radiates out to ask about the whole of one's life. Samuel Johnson's Idler 88, with Pliny's words as a title, comments, for instance, "This fatal question ['What have ye done?'] has disturbed the quiet of many other minds. He that in the latter part of his life too strictly enquires what he has done, can very seldom receive from his own heart such an account as will give him satisfaction."[5] The "wound" that the speaker is asking his loved one to be "patient" with here could be one's universal limitations as a human being, the damage of something like Original Sin, those elements of oneself that lead him to act in ways which require explanation or at least patience from those one loves.

The poems in *Intellectual Things* seem to be abstract and concerned with universals while those in *Passport to the War* are concrete and concerned with particulars. Kunitz himself has remarked that one of his "great influences was Plato, and I was very deep in Platonic lore . . . at this period of my first work." "Very Tree," one of the poems not reprinted from *Intellectual Things* in the 1944 volume, has as its theme, in Kunitz's added words, "the idea of tree, treeness as opposed to the shadow of the idea."[6] In the poem the poet rejects bark, leaves, a bird: "let there be/Only tree." Mostly, however, the Platonism in his first book is in the starting from generalities as in "Change" and "Geometry of Moods," the first two poems, or in "Motion of Wish" and "So Intricately Is This World Resolved," near the end of the book.

Partly no doubt the change between the two sets of poems came about as a result of experience and growth as well as the circumstances of the time. At least since the Romantics, poets have often seen themselves caught up in history, and, like Kunitz, young and not-so-young American men of the 1940s were more than most others snatched from their routines and lives and transported into another "curious life"—that of the drafted or enlisted. M. L. Rosenthal devotes several pages of the first chapter of his *New Poets*, a study of "American and British Poetry Since World War II," to "the deep, and literal, absorption of our age in the terrors of war . . ." and says,

War is more than a theme or subject for modern writers. It is a condition of consciousness, a destructive fact that explodes within the literature as without it. Just because the fact is so grossly obvious, we are in danger of overlooking its omnipresence.[7]

"The bloodied envelope addressed to you/Is history . . . ," Kunitz writes at the end of "Night Letter," and one has to emphasize the adjective "bloodied." A poet who is, in Kunitz's view, "more like others than anybody else,"[8] a representative man, can also more than others see himself *in* history. As Rosenthal says, so "the private life of the poet himself, especially under stress of psychological crisis, becomes a major theme. Often it is felt at the same time as a symbolic embodiment of national and cultural crisis."[9] In other words, "a gang of personal devils/. . . clank their jigging bones as public evils . . ." (SP, 113). Many of the new poems in *Passport to the War do* "clank their jigging bones as public evils. . . ." The full clarification of what Kunitz had to say, nonetheless, had to wait for the thematic grouping and rethinking that came fourteen years later with *Selected Poems*.

IV Selected Poems *(1958)*

The arrangement of the fifty-two poems from the first two books of poetry is completely discarded in *Selected Poems*, in which the earlier poems at no time maintain the same sequence. Thus it seems that Kunitz reexamined the relationships among his poems before "composing" this third book, which, as he says in his "Author's Note," are "in groups that bear some relevance to the themes, the arguments, that have preoccupied me since I began to write" (SP, front matter).

As noted below these groupings are made clear with titles taken from poems central to the sections; the five division titles are "The Serpent's Word," "The Terrible Threshold," "Prince of Counterfeits," "A World to Lose," and "The Coat without a Seam," each of them a highly figurative and suggestive phrase in itself.[10] The second of these section titles, "The Terrible Threshold," Kunitz used again as the title for his 1974 book of selected poems published in England (discussed in the next chapter).

The Serpent's Word. The first section, "The Serpent's Word," contains twenty-seven poems, more than half of them ones new in *Selected Poems*; the twin themes here are love and poetry. The section begins and ends with poems of the 1950s and includes in between a dozen poems from Kunitz's two earlier books. "The Dark and the Fair," from which the title of the section comes, in eight elegiac quatrains interrelates love and art (SP, 33–34).

The poem itself is a small archetypal drama: While the speaker is engaged in a heated discussion at a party, the Fair Lady, his present companion, comes to his side and puts in his hand her own "small impulsive" one, "Five-fingered gift." For him "The moment clanged . . . ," and he is reminded, like Marcel Proust tasting the madeleine soaked in tea, of the past: "risen from the past" the Dark Lady "eventually usurps the scene," Kunitz said in commenting on this poem.[11] Like the present Fair Lady, once years before the Dark Lady had similarly come to his side. "What brought her now, in the semblance of the warm," he asks in the sixth stanza, "Out of cold spaces, damned by colder blood?"

The Dark Lady had wronged him in that past time, and for her he had "killed the propitiatory bird . . . ," a sinful, symbolic action, apparently, like that of the Ancient Mariner. Now, though, "Peace to her bitter bones," he says in the last stanza, "Who taught me the serpent's word, but yet the word." Although the "word," given the association with "serpent," can be read as evil or the knowledge of good and evil, in the context of Kunitz's work as a whole, clearly it is poetry or this particular poem. From such hurtful experiences comes art.

Kunitz chose this poem as "a favorite or crucial poem"[12] from his own work for Engle and Langland's *Poet's Choice* (1962), saying that one of his reasons was that he liked "a poem that rides the beast of an action," and many of his strongest poems, like this one, do just that. "The Science of the Night," which opens this section and *Selected Poems*, so rides "the beast of an action," as does also "The Thief," the long, lively poem which closes "The Serpent's Word."

The Terrible Threshold. Most of the twenty-four poems in "The Terrible Threshold," section 2 of this book, are visionary, "religious" pieces from *Intellectual Things* with only four new poems and four from *Passport to the War*. Some of these are "Single Vision," "For the Word Is Flesh," "Father and Son," and the sonnet "So Intricately Is This World Resolved," all discussed above. "Open the Gates" (SP, 41), the short Blakean lyric from which the title of the section comes, is typical of the poems in "The Terrible Threshold." The three tetrameter quatrains, the "In Memoriam" stanza, present a strange action in which the naked "I" prowls through "the city of the burning cloud" dragging his life behind him in a sack. He knocks at a

door; the door opens, and he stands "on the terrible threshold" where
he sees "The end and the beginning in each other's arms."

Ralph J. Mills, Jr., points to the "nightmare effects" in this poem,
and I think "nightmare" sums up both this poem and many of the
other poems in this section. The "Gates" of the title may refer to
Penelope's story in the *Odyssey*, Book XIX, of the two gates of
dreams, the one of ivory for deceitful dreams, the other of horn for
prophetic dreams. The vision in this poem surely is that of the latter
kind; here as in another poem in this section he seems, prophetically,
to live all his life "at once" (SP, 51). The situation is similar to those in
"I Dreamed That I Was Old" and in "Change" (SP, 59 and 65):

> Here, Now, and Always, man would be
> Inviolate eternally:
> This is his spirit's trinity.   (SP, 65)

Prince of Counterfeits.   The third and middle section of *Selected
Poems*, "Prince of Counterfeits," has seventeen poems; only one of
them is from Kunitz's first book; nine are from *Passport to the War*,
and seven are new to this volume. The theme here is the treachery and
grief of the Self as singled out in such statements as "its own self turns
Christian-cannibal" and "The thing that eats the heart is mostly
heart" of the final poem in the section (SP, 71). In "My Surgeons" the
"I's" "butcher-boys" "cut" him up and squeeze out of his veins "The
bright liquor of sympathy. . . ."

> "No hope for persons any more,"
> They cry, "on either side of the grave."   (SP, 73)

The situation seems to be that as he matures the "I" sees what "the
world's game" (SP, 75) is, and he does not like it. A world of
disharmony, violence, and betrayal, it constantly imperils the Self. In
"The Guilty Man" the "I" says that "the darkness of the self goes
out/And spreads contagion on the flowing air." And what is it like in
the world?

> Heart against mouth is singing out of tune,
> Night's whisperings and blanks betrayed; this is
> The end of lies: my bones are angry with me.   (SP, 75)

By his title phrase, "The Guilty Man," Kunitz said, he does not "mean
someone who has sinned more than anybody else." Rather, he means

"the person who, simply by virtue of being mortal, is in a way condemned; he's mortal and he's fallible, and his life is inevitably a series of errors and consequences."[13]

This particular poem, then, "The Guilty Man," is an important one for Kunitz, perhaps a troublesome one, too, for he continued to revise it. In 1944 the last line was "None may forgive us for the ancient wrongs" (PW, 27). Possibly this phrasing seemed to point overmuch to Original Sin—an idea which certainly is in the poem—though, as Kunitz pointed out, it is there "Without the theological furniture."[14] At any rate for *Selected Poems* he altered it to "The souls of numbers kiss the perfect stars," a line of nearly baffling complexity (SP, 75). For the selection of his poems published in England in 1974, *The Terrible Threshold*, Kunitz extensively changed the final four lines of the poem moving them toward clarity and simplicity, also, I think, shifting the meaning somewhat, and leaving the poem less resolved— purposefully less resolved, it seems:

> I hate the excellence that spoils the world.
> So leave me now, you honorable men
> Whose treason is to turn the conscience kind,
> And do not turn until you hear a child. (pp. 16–17)

The poem from which the title of this section of *Selected Poems* comes, "The Fitting of the Mask," most explicitly outlines this implicit fable of the "treason" of the Self. A dialogue poem in eight stanzas, it has seven sestets rhyming abacbc; the seventh stanza, an italicized song, is eight lines, ababcbcb. The setting is a shop in which masks are sold, and the two speakers are a customer, the Self, who must have a mask to wear at the dance (of life, no doubt), and a merchant, a devil-figure. Two images which the customer would like he cannot buy and the one he is offered at the end he would rather not have seen. In the first line the Self says, "Again I come to buy the image fated" (SP, 82). The seller tells him that that image, "the youth, the undefeated," is gone. The customer chides the merchant for this and is given excuses.

"Enough!" the Self says in the third stanza; he will buy instead "another face," one described in the catalogue as "Fool of Love," clearly an image of another phase in the Self's life. The other protests that that mask is shopworn, and while rummaging around for yet another face, he sings a song about the various other faces that similarly cannot be sold: "*There's nothing left that's decent in our*

stock,/ And what are we to do, and what to do?" At last, however, he
finds another mask. "But look!" he says,

> "—here's something rare, macabre, a true
> Invention of the time's insomniac wits.
> Perhaps we ought to sell it to the zoo.
> Go to the darkening glass that traps your shames
> And tell me what you see."

"O Prince of Counterfeits," the customer cries in answer, "This is the
Self I hunted and knifed in dreams!"

A World to Lose. Section 4 of *Selected Poems,* "A World to Lose,"
has one new poem, "The Economist's Song," consistent in theme
and tone with the eight poems from *Passport to the War* that
complete the section. In a sense all nine poems are both political and
personal poems, the self horrified by what has happened but certain
too that he and everyone else are not without responsibility in the
catastrophe by which all are overtaken. "Our failures creep with
soldier hearts,/ Pointing their guns at what we love," the speaker says
in "The Last Picnic" (SP, 93), the first poem in the section and the one
from which the title of the section comes—"Yesterday we had a world
to lose."

In the meditative poem "Reflection by a Mailbox," waiting for the
postman to bring him his "passport to the war," presumably his draft
notice, the speaker reflects on the contemporary political situation—
Hitler, the Jewish persecution in Europe. His ancestors "step" from
his "American bones," he says, and he sees his immigrant parents,
"mother in a woven shawl,"

> . . . father picking up his pack
> For the return voyage through those dreadful years
> Into the winter of the raging eye.   (SP, 94)

His people, the Jews, are "game," he says, "For the hunters of man-
skins in the warrens of Europe . . . ," and he asks what it means:

> Are these the citizens of the new estate
> To which the continental shelves aspire;
> Or the powerful get of a dying age, corrupt
> And passion-smeared, with fluid on their lips,
> As if a soul had been given to petroleum?

How shall we uncreate that lawless energy?

In the final stanza he thinks "of Pavlov and his dogs/And the motto carved on the broad lintel of his brain:/'Sequence, consequence, and again consequence.'" And so these awful things, animalized humans, are not without their beginnings somewhere in our own selves.

The ironically titled poem "Careless Love" (SP, 95) which follows reflects on man's attraction to war in an extended conceit: soldiers "Are comforted by their guns . . . ," as though these instruments of killing were loved ones. Here war is a "nymphomaniac" and what she "enjoys/Inexhaustibly is boys." Similarly in "Confidential Instructions" (SP, 98) and "This Day This World," with diction and tone like those in some of Auden's satiric poems, the blame is put on man himself.

Closing the section, "Night Letter," one of Kunitz's best poems, brings all the elements together—"in the torment of our time," all are guilty, "self-accused," and suicidal. The sixty blank-verse lines of this dramatic monologue cannot be quoted in full, though they speak so clearly for themselves that one is tempted to do just that, or at least to quote three-quarters of them, as Ralph J. Mills, Jr., does in his discussion of the poem.[15]

The circumstances of "Night Letter" seem to be these: Away at the war "Night after night" the speaker tries to write to his beloved, but is beset instead by the horrors of his time. "Where is your ministry?" he asks, and adds,

> . . . I thought I heard
> A piece of laughter break upon the stair
> Like glass, but when I wheeled around I saw
> Disorder, in a tall magician's hat,
> Keeping his rabbit-madness crouched inside,
> Sit at my desk and scramble all the news.
> The strangest things are happening. Christ! the dead,
> Pushing the membrane from their face, salute
> The dead and scribble slogans on our walls;
> Phantoms and phobias mobilize, thronging
> The roads; and in the Bitch's streets the men
> Are lying down, great crowds with fractured wills
> Dumping the shapeless burden of their lives
> Into the rivers where the motors flowed.   (SP, 101)

"What have we done to them," he asks, "that what they are/Shrinks from the touch of what they hoped to be?" Out of his personal guilt,

"Pardon," he pleads, "clutching the fragile sleeve / Of my poor father's ghost returned to howl / His wrongs."

> I suffer the twentieth century,
> The nerves of commerce wither in my arm;
> Violence shakes my dreams; I am so cold,
> Chilled by the persecuting wind abroad,
> The oratory of the rodent's tooth,
> The slaughter of the blue-eyed open towns,
> And principle disgraced, and art denied.

As Mills says, this "hell of Kunitz's poem is a hell of our own invention, wherein we lock ourselves with greed, exploitation, and hatred of self and others."[16] This terrifying death-in-life that war, particularly, has brought us to, is conveyed through not only the vividness of the Mad Hatter image of Disorder but also that of the rising of the dead as they push "the membrane from their face," in a rebirth image. In addition, the simplicity of "I am so cold" is followed by what he is "Chilled by": "the persecuting wind," "The oratory of the rodent's tooth, / The slaughter of the blue-eyed open towns." The personification here, giving human "blue eyes" to "towns," works, I think, because of the connotations of childlike innocence and defenselessness in "blue-eyed" and "open" and as well the wartime meaning of an "open" city.[17]

After the abstract summation, "principle disgraced, and art denied," the speaker addresses his beloved simply, personally, as "My dear" and asks if it is "too late for us / To say, 'Let us be good unto each other'?" Then, emotion expended, in a peaceful few lines he sees

> The lamps go singly out; the valley sleeps;
> I tend the last light shining on the farms
> And keep for you the thought of love alive. . . .

His conclusion is that though this is a bad time for man, it is not the end of the world:

> Cities shall suffer siege and some shall fall,
> But man's not taken. What the deep heart means,
> Its message of the big, round, childish hand,
> Its wonder, its simple lonely cry,
> The bloodied envelope addressed to you,
> Is history, that wide and mortal pang.

This final "you" is no longer the beloved woman but all of us, man, and, as Kunitz says so often, "the deep heart," compassion, may yet save us if we but accept "The bloodied envelope addressed to" us. Although "Night Letter" is by no means an imitation of Arnold's "Dover Beach," or even necessarily influenced by it, that is the poem it most resembles in tone, subject, and resolution, and the two poems might profitably be read side by side. Both are nocturnal addresses to a beloved; the speakers are both shaken by the miseries and doubts of their time; and both poems find a refuge in love: "Ah, love, let us be true/To one another!" ("Dover Beach"), and "'Let us be good unto each other.'/... I tend the last light shining on the farms/And keep for you the thought of love alive ..." ("Night Letter").

The Coat without a Seam. The fifth and final section of *Selected Poems*, "The Coat without a Seam" is fittingly a strong one with only one poem each from each of Kunitz's previous volumes and six new poems, some of them the best in the collection. Three of these are fairly long poems with short lines—"The Way Down," seventy-two lines; "Revolving Meditation," seventy-four lines; and "A Spark of Laurel," thirty-six lines—a kind of poem new in Kunitz's work and a kind of poem, too, that becomes increasingly characteristic. He commented himself that as time went on his "line has been getting shorter, partly because I'm cutting down on adjectives—I'm usually down to two or three stresses to a line. This permits any number of syllables, within reason, as long as the ground pattern is preserved."[18] These short-lined poems themselves, like the other poems in this section, are poems about poetry or art. In "The Way Down" the action seems to be an archetypal allegory of a journey through time, a descent and a return. "Time swings her burning hands," and the "I" sees an unspecified "him going down .../To a cabin underground/Where his hermit father lives. ..." His hermit father's coat is "The coat without a seam" of the title phrase, the coat

> That the race, in its usury, bought
> For the agonist to redeem,
> By dying in it, one
> Degree a day till the whole
> Circle's run.   (SP, 106)

These lines connect "The coat without a seam" to both Adam and Christ as in John's gospel, yet Kunitz appears not to be using the phrase in its strict theological meaning;[19] rather the coat is a magical garment symbolical of unity as such a remarkably woven piece of clothing easily can be. In the second stich the "I" dies at the same time as "the magician," but then revives. "Must I learn again to breathe?" he asks, and everything wakes with him. Finally, in section 3 he asks his "father in the wood,/Mad father of us all" to "Receive your dazzling child/Drunk with the morning-dew/Into your fibrous love. . . ."

Too explicit explaining of the allegory might detract from the poem, though one can say at least that it touches on the poetic process, the necessity of knowing one's depths, and is in the tranced poet tradition of Coleridge's poet in "Kubla Khan":

> His flashing eyes, his floating hair!
> Weave a circle round him thrice,
> And close your eyes with holy dread,
> For he on honeydew hath fed,
> And drunk the milk of Paradise.

Besides, the poem does what Kunitz has said he likes a poem to do; it "rides the beast of an action," a descent in this case. As he explained to inquiring students in a biographical aside, he could not expect them "to know that I began to write the poem after making the steep descent down to the Grotto of Neptune in Tivoli, not far from Rome."[20] Yet the physical details of the poem are specific enough for readers to infer a physical setting, the quite specific "miracle" of sewing a "coat without a seam," with the Apollo, Christ, and father images making up the backbone of the poem. Still, "The actual physical setting," as Kunitz went on to say, "is of no consequence, for 'the way down' of the poem is into a mythic underground, older than self or history. Down there the protagonist confronts the mystery of his roots, endures his fate, and is restored to life."[21]

The dithyrambic force of the poem comes across partly through the form, that of the Cowleyan or irregular ode, suitable to the exalted rapture of the material: here quick six-syllabled lines in the first and third numbered parts, mostly longer lines in part 2, and irregular rhyming. "Hands," at the end of the first line, for example, links with "lands" in line three; but "down" of line 2 is not echoed until line 9 when it is repeated. "Gold" of line 4 has no rhyme, but lines 5–8 are alternately rhymed—"specked," "mind," "crack," "grind"—a pattern of rhyme recurring here and there throughout the poem to give an overall highly musical effect.

Three of the other poems in this final part of *Selected Poems*, like "The Thief" in the first section, are uncharacteristically (for Kunitz) relaxed and even exuberant—"The Class Will Come to Order," "A Choice of Weapons," and "Revolving Meditation." In the first of these, one of Kunitz's most engaging poems, the speaker walks on a college campus prior to a class. He has received a letter from his beloved, from whom he is temporarily separated, and the thought of love and the feel of this letter in his pocket give him joy; later in the classroom he smiles to himself but does not tell his students why he smiles.

The poem has two epigraphs, an unusual practice for Kunitz, one from Joyce's *Finnegans Wake* and another from Dante's *Vita Nuova*. They set the academic scene and prepare for some of the content of the poem.

O tell me all about Anna Livia! I want to hear all about Anna Livia. Well, you know Anna Livia? Yes, of course, we all know Anna Livia. Tell me all. Tell me now. You'll die when you hear.

. . . *ed io sorridendo li guardava, e nulla dicea loro.*   (SP, 110)

That he has his own tale to tell runs through the poem, as do also allusions to Joyce, who is familiarly dubbed "Our Irish friend," "old father," and "Artificer." The Dante quotation is paraphrased in the last two lines of the poem (Dante: "I, smiling, looked at them and said nothing" [22]).

The speaker begins by describing what is around him in a playful tone.

> Amid that Platonic statuary, of athletes
> Playing their passionate and sexless games,
> The governors-to-be struck careless on the lawns,
> The soldiers' monument, the sparrow-bronzes,
> Through that museum of Corinthian elms
> I walked among them in the
> Soliloquy of summer, a gravel-scholar.

The speaker's own soliloquy runs over Joyce's phrase "silence, exile, and cunning": he will himself be silent—"not . . . the silence of the cowed,/ But hold your tongue, sir, rather than betray." Silent, he can then

> . . . hear a music not prescribed, a tendril-tune
> That climbs the porches of the ear,
> Green, cool, like cucumber-vine.
> What if the face starts threatening the man?
> Then exile, cunning.

This last line, neatly sliced in half by the caesura, goes on,

> Yes, old father, yes,
> The newspapers were right,
> Youth is general all over America. . . .

With this turn on Joyce's words at the end of "The Dead," the concluding story of *Dubliners*—"Yes, the newspapers were right: snow was general all over Ireland."—the "I" of the poem thinks of the snow and the westward journey in that story and quotes his beloved's words in the letter:

> "The almonds bloom," she wrote. But will they hold,
> While I remain to teach the alphabet
> I still must learn, the alphabet on fire,
> Those wizard stones? As always, where the text ends
> Lurks the self, so shamed and magical. Away!

This "Away!" at the end of this last line could echo Stephen's two "Away's" at the end of *A Portrait of the Artist as a Young Man*, as Stephen's in turn possibly echoes Keats's in "Ode to a Nightingale," bringing in some of the "magical" atmosphere of that poem:

> Away! Away! for I will fly to thee,
> Not charioted by Bacchus and his pards,
> But on the viewless wings of Poesy.

Kunitz's line itself, with a terminal caesura like other lines in the poem, has a colloquial rhythm and force partly because of the high proportion of monosyllables. The line that follows, "Who stays here long enough will stay too long," is monosyllabic except for the middle word, "enough," and it balances speech stress and metrical stress; Harvey Gross has noted that the final lines of the poem similarly do so ("I smiled . . .").[23]

The speaker prefers change and disorder to the order of the academy. "Time snaps her fan, and there's her creature caught. . . ."

He introduces the important lines of the poem with a foreshortened trimeter line followed by six pentameters:

> Absurd though it may seem, [trimeter]
> Perhaps there's too much order in this world;
> The poets love to haul disorder in,
> Braiding their wrists with her long mistress hair,
> And when the house is tossed about our ears,
> The governors must set it right again.
> How wise was he who banned them from his state!

Clearly the "I" is thinking about his own roles as teacher and poet, the subverting of the order of the world. As Kunitz comments in an essay, "Plato . . . felt that the right words for the poet might be the wrong words for the state," and when he "banned" poets "from his state" he specified, Kunitz rightly insists, that he had

nothing against poets . . . content to exercise their craft by writing hymns to the gods and praises of famous men. The poets to guard against are those who nourish the passions and desires. These are the sons of Dionysus, the god of wine and ecstasy, as opposed to the rulers of the state, who are sons of Apollo, a relatively moderate divinity.[24]

The speaker of the poem could toss the house about the ears of his students should he choose to tell his tale, as he feels he is asked to do in the chiming line "O tell me a tale before the lecture-bell!" fashioned on the epigraph from Joyce. In the classroom, he invokes Joyce, as Daedalus, in an alliterative, mostly monosyllabic epizeuxis (doubling words for emphasis: "I swear"), "I swear, Artificer, I swear I saw/Their souls awaiting me, with notebooks primed." He continues with a crucial question:

> The lesson for today, the lesson's what?
> I must have known, but did not care to know.
> There is a single theme, the heart declares,
> That circumnavigates curriculum.
> The letter in my pocket kissed my hand.
> I smiled but I did not tell them,
> I did not tell them why it was I smiled.

Concluding the poem these last four lines individually deserve attention: "The letter in my pocket kissed my hand" for its everyday

simplicity metaphorically lifted up by the substitution of "kissed" for
the expected "touched" and for the reversal of the actual, which
would be "My hand touched the letter. . . ." The final two lines
paraphrase the Dante epigraph and, doubling again for emphasis,
another epizeuxis ("I did not tell them,/I did not tell them. . . ."),
begin and end with the same words ("I smiled").

Then, finally, "circumnavigates curriculum," nine syllables in two
words, verb and object, surrounded by less weighty words, has a
whole verbal and visual humor that is consistent with the rest of the
poem. "But hold your tongue, sir, rather than betray./Decorum is a
face the brave can wear . . . ," for instance, and "The poets love to
haul disorder in . . ."—both of these begin with colloquial diction
("hold your tongue," "love to haul") and rhythm and continue with
consciously formal, "poetic," elegant phrases. After "to haul disorder
in" comes "Braiding their wrists with her long mistress hair," a play
on Donne's "celebrated line from *The Relique*," as Harvey Gross
says: "A bracelet of bright hair about the bone." Kunitz's line here,
Gross further notes, has a "sinuous beauty . . . produced by the
strategically place short *i*'s as well as by the reversed first foot and the
double foot standing in the third and fourth positions." [25]

An accomplished prosodist, Kunitz shows his skill perhaps
nowhere so clearly as in this line and generally throughout this light-
hearted, felicitous blank-verse poem. Each of the four poems that
follow "The Class Will Come to Order" in *Selected Poems*, however,
is similarly varied in prosody and diction. In the eight lines of "The
Summing-Up" the high proportion of monosyllables speeds reading
as the relaxed diction—"scribbled," "cheap," "my gear," "damn the
cost!"—lightens the portentousness of its content and of some of the
heavier words ("disburdened," "ransomed," "lintel"):

> When young I scribbled, boasting, on my wall,
> No Love, No Property, No Wages.
> In youth's good time I somehow bought them all,
> And cheap, you'd think, for maybe a hundred pages.
>
> Now in my prime, disburdened of my gear,
> My trophies ransomed, broken, lost,
> I carve again on the lintel of the year
> My sign: *Mobility*—and damn the cost!   (SP, 112)

In "A Choice of Weapons" witty feminine rhymes ("elation-reputa-
tion," "devils-evils," "empiric-lyric," "folly-melancholy," "garden-

harden") convey a teasing tone; and in "Revolving Meditation" the diction, especially, makes its grave material readable: the pleasant colloquialism of "God knows," "a sprig or two," "in a nutshell," or "this perjured quid of mine" (SP, 114–15).

Along with "A Spark of Laurel" these are the fine new poems with which *Selected Poems* ends. Harvey Gross noted Kunitz's maintenance of "iambic discipline" up to this point; subsequently Kunitz began publishing in journals poems in freer meters. Gross points to "The Mound-Builders," published in 1963, five years later, as a poem "written in a free meter very close to Lowell's." [26] In a long review article published the year after *Selected Poems*, Kunitz noted that his own age happened "*not* to be a time of great innovation in poetic technique; it is rather a period in which the technical gains of past decades, particularly the 'twenties, are being tested and consolidated." [27] Now this testing and consolidating he was doing himself, having, possibly, "exhausted," as he has said, the potentialities of strict forms.

"As one matures and changes, the voice must change too," Kunitz said in an interview in 1968. "It cannot remain the voice of a young man of twenty-five when you are sixty." In his own case, he added, he noticed that he was "moving toward a much more open style. . . . I somehow no longer feel right within a tight structure, and I'm trying to crack it." [28] How he achieved this "cracking" of "a tight structure," his next and fourth book, *The Testing-Tree*, shows.

CHAPTER 5

Through Dark and Deeper Dark: 1971 and 1974 Books of Poetry

TWO more of Kunitz's books of poetry are *The Testing-Tree* (1971) and *The Terrible Threshold* (1974), published in England. The second of these books, in the series of Secker and Warburg Poets, contains no new poems; the new arrangements of poems from the three immediately preceding works make, however, for a notably different "interior logic," and so *The Terrible Threshold* will be examined below briefly after a consideration of *The Testing-Tree*.

I The Testing-Tree *(1971)*

In the thirty poems of *The Testing-Tree* Kunitz "surpasses himself," Robert Lowell wrote in a note reprinted on the book jacket: "the old iron [is] brought to a white heat of simplicity." When the book appeared in 1971 Kunitz was just past his mid-sixties, and in the thirteen years since *Selected Poems* he had been writing poems different from any that he had written before—different in form, most of all, but also changed in diction and to some extent in subject matter. Lowell's further remark, "Call no man old, who can grow," though a trifle supererogatory, touches on the principal importance of these new poems. What are the signs of "growth"? Free meters; syntactic relaxation; at times elimination of punctuation; the dropping of conventional line capitalization; and often the lack of stanzaic structure and rhyme.

Interior Logic. The book is divided into four numbered, untitled parts and has three pages of notes at the end. Kunitz was into his sixty-seventh year in 1971, and the three pages of notes make the

86

pagination exactly that, sixty-seven. The first section has poems of contemporary reference, "Journal for My Daughter" and "The Flight of Apollo," and is, primarily, in Kunitz's words, "the overture, anticipating the main themes." But the "interior logic" of this book, he says, is "less definite" than that in *Selected Poems*. He "shuffled" these poems "all around." Mainly, "Section two is dominated by poems of place," according to Kunitz; "three, political; four deals with the role and character of the artist."[1] This final part, a collection of ten "artist" poems, three of them translations of Anna Akhmatova, the great contemporary Russian poet, brings up the question of the inclusion of translations in this volume of Kunitz's own poetry.

The seven translations are here, Kunitz said, first because he "liked them as poems," and second

... because they seemed to have an affinity with my own work. ... These few translations seemed to me to fit into the logic of this particular book. I deliberately excluded scores of others.[2]

Two of these translations are in part II of *The Testing-Tree* along with other "poems of place," Osip Mandelstam's "Summer Solstice" and "Tristia"; two others are in III, the section of political poems, Yevtushenko's "Hand-Rolled Cigarettes" and Aba Stolzenberg's "Bolsheviks"; and three are those in the fourth and final section of the book, the artist group, Akhmatova's "Boris Pasternak," "Dante," and "Cleopatra."

Without these translations part IV would have seven poems, I and II six each, and III four original poems. So summed up and even read through the first time, *The Testing-Tree* might seem a slight collection. Rereading it, though, one finds it enlarged by the quality and depth of the poems: surprising ones such as "King of the River" and "The Magic Curtain," probing ones like "Journal for My Daughter" and the title poem, and startling ones like "Robin Redbreast" and "The Mulch." And overall the Kunitz of this book is, in a sense, a "new" Kunitz, one who has grown and changed in the thirteen years since *Selected Poems*. He has grown older, wiser, more compassionate, and is more direct and emotionally moving than ever before. As Stanley Moss said in his review of the book, here Kunitz's "self, poetry and nature are worked with as one consubstantial stuff," an "accomplishment," Moss added, that "should occasion a national holiday."[3]

The Wounds of Life. How did this considerable "accomplishment," this "growth" come about? To such a question there is no one answer, for such change no one explanation. Biographically we can note the importance of Kunitz's enormously successful tour of the Soviet Union in 1967—and here at home, his revisiting of past sites important to him. In April 1971, when he read at the Worcester Poetry Festival at the Worcester Library, he reportedly "mentioned how, for many years after leaving the city, he drove miles out of the way to avoid it."[4] He doubts, he said, that he will ever "forget Worcester," the city of his birth, it had so "scarred" him.[5] Once back in Worcester, though, he "looked," he has written, "for the old house at the city's edge and those Indian woods" that he had roamed in as a boy.

The place had turned into a technological nightmare . . . an express highway running through my childhood. On the site of my nettled field stood a housing development ugly enough for tears.

This "depressing adventure" was "one reason why I had to write 'The Testing-Tree.'"[6]

Through this poem (TT, 60–63) and the others in the volume runs a sense of moral strength and survival. The earlier themes and attitudes of savage indignation and outrage seem mostly replaced by a direct facing of the facts of life, one of them, as David Huddle has noted, "the terrible fact of his growing old. . . ."[7]

> It is necessary to go
> through dark and deeper dark
> and not to turn.   (TT, 63)

"What's best in me lives underground," Kunitz says in "The Mound Builders," "rooting and digging, itching for wings . . ." (TT, 45). "Kunitz's language *ruthlessly* prods the wounds of his life," Stanley Moss notes (my italics). "Yet nowhere in the fiber of this book," Moss adds, "is there a thread of malice, anger, hatred, envy, pique; not a sneer, not a 'sidelong pickerel smile,' nor does Kunitz turn the other cheek."[8] This last observation of Moss's should be stressed lest it seem that these are poems of serene old age. As Kunitz says in the opening poem, the "folded message in his hands" reads,

> *What do I want of my life?*
> *More! More!*   (TT, 6)

Poems which particularly "ruthlessly prod . . . the wounds of his life" are "Journal for My Daughter," and as well "The Illumination," "The Portrait," "King of the River," "River Road," and "Robin Redbreast." The first (TT, 3–7), one of Kunitz's longest poems, 145 lines, is an unrhymed lyric in nine numbered sections. A poem of recollection and meditation, it begins with two sections of summary: the father, separated from his daughter, sees "A popeyed chipmunk," "field mice," and "the needle-nosed shrew" gathering in supplies for the winter, a metaphor for life:

> I propose
> that we gather our affections.
> Lambkin, I care.

Sections 3 to 5 are reminiscences about his happiness at her birth, his walking the floor with her when she cried as a baby, and her crawling under a sofa during a visit from "a big blond uncle-bear," a Roethke-figure. In the next two sections he follows her growing up; in part 7 he pictures her during a student demonstration, approving of her activity as consistent in the "flinty maverick line" of their family heritage.

In the eighth section he remembers the death and burial of her first dog, "the summer I went away," and his carrying her outdoors to watch her first eclipse. This leads directly into the anecdote about Coleridge which makes up the short, single-sentenced final section:

> The night when Coleridge,
> heavy-hearted,
> bore his crying child outside,
> he noted
> that those brimming eyes
> caught the reflection
> of the starry sky,
> and each suspended tear
> made a sparkling moon.

Since this image ends the long poem, clearly Kunitz is commenting on the importance of his daughter's tears, her sorrows to him.[9]

The sense of loss, regret, waste, and misunderstanding in this poem is made explicit in the next one, "The Illumination" (TT, 8–9), a lyric of mystical insight and paradox in which a Dante-Christ figure appears to the poet. The narrative, action, dialogue, images, and such

things as the hotel and the crosslike key work together to make the
stark, almost adjectiveless thirty short lines of the poem compact with
meaning and emotion beyond its brevity. The scene is a hotel room:

> In that hotel my life
> rolled in its socket
> twisting my strings.

Then all his "mistakes" from his "earliest/bedtimes," rise against him:

> the parent I denied,
> the friends I failed,
> the hearts I spoiled,
> including at least
> my own left ventricle—
> a history of shame.

In a shattering dream moment the persona cries, "'Dante!' . . . /to
the apparition/entering from the hall,/laureled and gaunt,/in a cone
of light." To this vision, he says,

> "Out of mercy you came
> to be my Master
> and my guide!"
> To which he [Dante] replied:
> "I know neither the time
> nor the way
> nor the number on the door . . .
> but this must be my room,
> I was here before."
> And he held up in his hand
> the key
> which blinded me.[10]

In the poem the emotion mounts up to the twenty-ninth and next-to-
the-last line, "the key," which, isolated, seems "held up" on the page,
an effect to which the largely nominal preceding lines greatly
contribute. I count twenty-seven nouns including the proper noun
"Dante" and only two descriptive adjectives, "laureled and gaunt";
the other adjectives, aside from "earliest" and "left," are demonstra-
tives and possessives. The result is an unembellished poem of terror
and power.

The lost father still haunts the poet in *The Testing-Tree*. In this poem, "The Illumination," he is no doubt "the parent I denied. . . ." In another the speaker sings "and father I had none" (TT, 58). In "Three Floors" he sees his "father flying;/the wind was walking on my neck,/the windowpanes were crying" (TT, 10). In "The Portrait" in his "sixty-fourth year" he deals directly with his father's suicide without dream disguise or fable.

> My mother never forgave my father
> for killing himself,
> especially at such an awkward time
> and in a public park,
> that spring
> when I was waiting to be born.
> She locked his name
> in her deepest cabinet
> and would not let him out,
> though I could hear him thumping.   (TT, 57)

The crucial incident from his childhood is his finding a picture of his father in the attic, possibly in the "wardrobe trunk" mentioned in "Three Floors," "whose lock a boy could pick. . . ." When he came down to his mother

> with the pastel portrait in my hand
> of a long-lipped stranger
> with a brave mustache
> and deep brown level eyes,
> she ripped it into shreds
> without a single word
> and slapped me hard.

In quiet, undecorated lines of diminishing lengths (6, 5, and 3 syllables) the poem ends powerfully:

> In my sixty-fourth year
> I can feel my cheek
> still burning.

Its clarity and unsparing omission of judgment make the poem a judgment in itself. About a "pastel portrait" of a "stranger," his father, it is a portrait of his mother who, caught up in her own tangled emotions, deprived her son of her memories of his father.

"King of the River" (TT, 15–17), too, "prods the wounds" of life, here more philosophically trying to answer questions about life, age, and death. The starting point for this particular observation is the fact, as Kunitz says in his note, that

Within two weeks after leaving the ocean to swim up the rivers of the Northwest and spawn, the bounding Pacific salmon degenerates into "an aged, colorless, and almost lifeless fish." The same geriatric process in humans takes some twenty to forty years. (TT, 65)

And so in the guise of the struggle of the salmon going upstream the poet is describing the mental and physical state he is presently in: "The great clock of our life/is slowing down,/and the small clocks run wild." The line is reminiscent of the clocks implicit at the end of "The Science of the Night": "Each cell within my body holds a heart/And all my hearts in unison strike twelve." They strike a late hour now indeed.

The fourth and final section of the poem makes especially clear the present state of stoic endurance:

> If the heart were pure enough,
> but it is not pure,
> you would admit
> that nothing compels you
> any more, nothing
> at all abides,
> but nostalgia and desire,
> the two-way ladder
> between heaven and hell. (TT, 16–17)

The second sentence of this section continues this reflection and ends the poem:

> On the threshold
> of the last mystery,
> at the brute absolute hour,
> you have looked into the eyes
> of your creature self,
> which are glazed with madness,
> and you say
> he is not broken but endures,
> limber and firm
> in the state of his shining,
> forever inheriting his salt kingdom,
> from which he is banished
> forever.

Like that of the salmon the poet's final position in this poem is one of paradoxical stasis, "forever inheriting his salt kingdom,/from which he is banished/forever." The two "forever's" surround the "salt kingdom," physically and figuratively—for the salmon the Pacific, for man his young and middle years. The "poignance here," David Huddle has said, "is very nearly unbearable in the emotional context of the poem: that the human condition is such that a man forever inherits that from which he is forever banished."[11]

The use of the second person ("you," "yourself") for the persona gives "King of the River" a hard, unpitying universality which the more usual, personal first ("I," "me") could not have conveyed. The two exceptions are in the two important quoted cries of wind and fire: "'I did not choose the way,/the way chose me.'"; "'Burn with me!/The only music is time, the only dance is love.'" Like the "Finned Ego" of the first sentence of the poem, "the way," burning, "music," "time," "dance," and "love" of these quotations have for the reader significances beyond themselves. As Stanley Moss remarks, "It is not by chance that 'Finned Ego' is capitalized. Something of the great 'I AM' must dart through the reader's mind. The poem aches for the unknowable, the unattainable."[12]

The rhetorical organization of the poem reinforces this philosophical grasping: conditional statements ("If") are followed by contrasting "but's" in each of the four principal sections:

> If the water were clear enough,
> if the water were still,
> but the water is not clear,
> the water is not still. . . .

In the second verse paragraph it is "If the knowledge were given you,/but it is not given"; in the third, "If the power were granted you"; in the fourth, "If the heart were pure enough . . ."—the movement from "water" to "knowledge" to "power" to "heart" charts the circling-in of the meaning of the poem.

In "River Road" (TT, 30–31), a fragment of autobiography, the time is "the eve of war," "That year of the cloud," when his "marriage failed," and the action is that of a ritual planting. The "I" planted "red pine and white, larch, balsam fir,/one stride apart, two hundred to the row. . . ." The first two of the three sections of the poem each begin with the same line, "That year of the cloud, when my marriage failed" and deal with, first, the recollection, then, the planting. In the

third, the last section, it is the passage of the years since then; time can
be measured by the growth of the trees, then mere fantails "of
squirming roots/that kissed the palm of my dirty hand"; now grown
tall, old, they make "woods."

Returning to this former place of his "on the river road," he asks,
"Lord! Lord! who has lived so long?/Count it ten thousand trees
ago,/five houses and ten thousand trees. . . ." The final juxtaposition
is a placing of his walking into the woods he had made, "his dark and
resinous, blistered land," beside a return to the past—"through the
deep litter of the years," both a real and a metaphorical walk.

The game in the twelve lines of "The Game," the expressive
allegory that ends *The Testing-Tree*, is both the childhood "game" of
"spin the bottle" and the "game" of life, suggesting the similarity
between the chances in the game as to which way the bottle may point
and those in life. The second and third of the two-lined stanzas
concern the onset of age with the fourth rising to metaphysics and the
fifth to a cry—

> O the night is coming on
> And I am nobody's son

The solace is, finally, "Father it's true/But only for a day. . . ."
Formally, "The Game" stands apart from the other poems in the
book: it is the only poem which is unpunctuated and also the only one
in which each line begins with a capital letter in the old way. Its
brevity, simplicity of structure, and effective diction give it the feeling
of a nursery rhyme or a coda, the point to which one comes after
going "through dark and deeper dark. . . ."

Versification in The Testing-Tree.   Kunitz calls the "system" he uses
in this book "functional stressing" and explains its restrictions: first,
he has

a music haunting my ear . . . that's one limitation; secondly, in writing what
may look like free verse I have a system of strong beats in mind. In recent
years my line has been getting shorter. . . . I'm . . . down to two or three
stresses to a line. This permits any number of syllables, within reason, as long
as the ground pattern is preserved.[13]

Both "The Illumination" and "The Portrait" are functionally stressed
as are others in *The Testing-Tree* such as "The Mulch," the title poem,

and "River Road." The four sentences of "The Portrait," for instance, are arranged in twenty-one lines with each line a phrase with no separation of adjective from noun or of conjunction and preposition from its phrase. Each line ends either in a noun, as fifteen lines do, or in commas and periods, as eight lines do, and hence the poem, its "ground pattern . . . preserved," has the simplicity and exactness of good prose and the purposive grace of good "free" verse.

In "River Road" the fifty-one lines are mostly eight, nine, or ten syllables, again primarily phrasal with only occasionally a separation of parts that naturally go together. One example of a noun parted from its adjective is "one night saw a Hessian soldier/stand at attention there in full/regalia, till his head broke into flames." The positioning of "full" at the end of one line and "regalia" at the beginning of the next makes for an effect suitable to the odd apparition.

Still, the "abandonment" in this book of the "iambic discipline" that Harvey Gross noted as characteristic of Kunitz's earlier verse does not all the same mean a shunning of stanzaic forms. The long sections of "The Magic Curtain," the poem at the center of *The Testing-Tree*, for example, are arranged in quatrains of combined ten- and eight-syllabled lines while those in the title poem are in phrasal triads. The verse of one of the several love poems in this book, "After the Last Dynasty" (TT, 28–29), is like that in "The Portrait," suited to its matter, here that of the faithless Early Lady, she with her "small bad heart," she who "failed" him, and fought him with her weakness and sickness, not with her strength and health. "Pet, spitfire, blue-eyed pony," he addresses her tenderly in the second and last section of the thirty-eight-line poem,

> here is a new note
> I want to pin on your door,
> though I am ten years late
> and you are nowhere:
> Tell me,
> are you still mistress of the valley,
> what trophies drift downriver,
> why did you keep me waiting?

Similarly the form of "King of the River" is "freer" than was usual in Kunitz's earlier poems. In the first section the first nine lines contract from eight syllables to two, then expand to five, move back to three for the important phrase "Finned Ego," out to six, back to two, like more and more rapid intake and outflow of one's breath, a line that "coils,/uncoils." The phrasal arrangement is the consistent pattern in the other sections, too, with most lines five, six, or eight syllables long, and only three out of the total seventy-eight lines in the poem longer. The longest and hence the most emphatic line is the third one from the end, the eleven-syllabled "forever inheriting his salt kingdom. . . ."

Yet another poem "Indian Summer at Land's End" (TT, 24), without rhyme, has an almost blank-verse formality. The caesura, for example, is mainly after the fourth, fifth, and sixth syllables, that is, medial as in traditional caesural practice for ten-syllabled lines, and so the twenty lines of the poem have a strict dignity of form. The speaker longs for his loved one, the Later Lady, who, absent from him, he dreams of as with him. As in "The Science of the Night," the mature love poem that opened *Selected Poems*, in this one he pictures sleep as a voyage, here a voyage on the sea, not in space.

> Last night I reached for you and shaped you there
> lying beside me as we drifted past
> the farthest seamarks and the watchdog bells,
> and round Long Point throbbing its frosty light,
> until we streamed into the open sea.
> What did I know of voyaging till now?

These six lines in the middle of the poem, along with the final line, are the only ones in the poem without punctuational caesuras. So singled out in positions and meaning as different from the other lines, they are also in positions and meanings central in the poem. It is a long, almost unbroken voyage, that of this night. The poem itself concludes with a shortened line and four periods of ellipsis, drifting off, unfinished, continuing . . .

> . . . the southbound Canada express
> hoots of horizons and distances. . . .

The central poem of the book, "The Magic Curtain," has a markedly different form. The title suggests a turn on "the magic lantern," an early term for the projected still pictures that developed into the motion picture and also an allusion to the theater "curtain" that used to rise or part to begin a showing. Of course the phrase has other connotations, too, the "magical" life of early childhood and curtains of various other kinds.

The "I" of the poem, called "Sonny," dressed in a "starched white sailor suit/and buttoned shoes," must be six or seven years old. Frieda, his "first love," is a German servant girl employed in his household, a "capricious keeper of the toast. . . ." Instead of Sonny's going to school, the two of them dream away the day at the Bijou and Majestic nickelodeons. The second numbered section of the poem particularizes details from early movies, those of Pauline and her perils, the Keystone Kops, Charlie Chaplin, and the films of D. W. Griffith. Kunitz himself counts his seeing "nearly every early movie that was made" an important part of his education, second after "the Indian-haunted woods behind" his home, and before the public library and the Worcester Classical High School.[14]

This long poem conveys well a past time and a past experience, "first love," that for Frieda and that for the movies, and makes an extended analogy in the third section between life itself and the movies.

> Let the script revel in tricks and transformations.
> When the film is broken, let it be spliced
> where Frieda vanished one summer night
> with somebody's husband, daddy to a brood.
> And with her vanished, from the bureau drawer,
> the precious rose-enameled box
> that held those chestnut-colored curls
> clipped from my sorrowing head when I was four.

The numbers in Frieda's counting song in the first section had gone forward, "*Eins, zwei, drei, vier*," but in the final section here they go "backward, see!/The operator's lost control." "Your story," your life, is a film that spills

> in a montage on a screen,
> with chases, pratfalls, custard pies, and sores.
> You have become your past, which time replays,
> to your surprise, as comedy.

The italicized counting song, in English now, not German, moves from "Five" to "one," similarly backward.

Consisting of six, eight, and seven groups of unrhymed quatrains, the three sections of the poem give order to the eighty-four lines.

Within the quatrains the syllable count usually runs 10, 8, 8, and 10
with no syntactical runover from quatrain to quatrain. In the line
"riddles, nonsense, lieder, counting-songs. . . ." (1. 16), the four
periods at the end function as a syllable to make the line look ten-
syllabled. And so, too, in line 57, "Five . . . four . . . three . . . two . . .
one . . .": each of the five sets of three periods can be a syllable. In the
italicized song in section three the periods have been reduced to two
but again act as a syllable each:

> *Five . . four . . three . . two . . one . .*
> *Where has my dearest gone?*
> *She is nowhere to be found,*
> *She dwells in the underground.*

Such use of this device of periods is typical of the craft of "The Magic
Curtain," which at the same time never departs from easygoing,
idiomatic clarity. In the last line of the poem the "I" says what Frieda
meant to him, simply, repetitively. His mother will " 'never forgive
her,' " for having run off "with somebody's husband," taking with her
the box containing Sonny's curls. Sonny, though, says, "as for me, I
do and do and do."

"Life Aims at the Tragic. . . ."   Many of the poems in *The Testing-
Tree* treat of the savagery of life with a humor and irony which save
them from what might otherwise be an excessive bitterness. "The
Magic Curtain" notes, for instance, "You have become your past,
which time replays,/to your surprise, as comedy." And, as in
slapstick comedy or nightmare, "That coathanger neatly whisked
your coat/right off your back. Soon it will want your skin." A similar
savage irony pervades "An Old Cracked Tune," a poem modeled on
the anti-Semitic song about a Jewish tailor, "Solomon Levi," which,
improbable though it seems now, in my time was lustily sung in
schools.[15] In that poem the second of the two stanzas reads:

> The sands whispered, *Be separate,*
> the stones taught me, *Be hard.*
> I dance, for the joy of surviving,
> on the edge of the road.   (TT, 58)

More than any of the other poems in the book, though, perhaps the
adaptation of lines from Naum Korzhavin, which Kunitz entitles

"The Bottom of the Glass" and considers an "imitation," not a translation, gives this aspect of the Kunitz of *The Testing-Tree*:

> Not by planning and not by choosing
> I learned the mastery.
> What a damnable trade
> where winning is like losing!
> The wheel keeps spinning,
> the thread gets broken,
> my hand cannot tell
> its work from its loafing.
> Life aims at the tragic:
> what makes it ridiculous?
> In age as in youth
> the joke is preposterous.
> And nothing shall save me
> from meanness and sinning
> but more of the same,
> more losing like winning.   (TT, 56)

"I lost by winning, and I shall not win/ Again except by loss" of "Postscript," a 1930 poem (SP, 16–17), are lines similar in idea but without the simplicity and hardness of these sixteen short lines. Here the feminine rhymes, paradoxical meanings, and reverberating metaphorical title apparently present drinking as a metaphor for life, with puns on "trade" (both an occupation and an exchange) and "glass" (a drinking container and a mirror). The "winning" in drinking and living is getting to "the bottom of the glass," in effect, "losing," since the alcohol and time are gone. One exchanges in life the tragic for the ridiculous, a distorting mirror image.

Comic diction is deliberately employed in the first part of "The Mound Builders" (TT, 45–46), the long, serious poem meditating about "The civilization . . . [which] flourished between A.D. 900 and 1100" in Georgia (TT, 66). The leaders in Washington are "geezers" who "jig," and the poet himself, "knee-deep in South" and "oiled by Methodist money," whirls "to a different music. . . ." In his "rented Falcon" he "flies/from the tiresome sound of my own voice,/the courteous chicken sitting on my plate,/and Sidney Lanier's exhausted flute/stuck in its cabinet of glass." "Macon is the seventh layer of civilization on this spot," the epigraph says smugly, and after seriously considering the mound builders in section 2, the poet ends the poem with six lines of summary, the flourish of rhyme, and a humorous thrust:

> The mounds rise up on every side
> of a seven-layered world, as I stand
> in the middle of the Ocmulgee fields,
> by the Central of Georgia Railway track,
> with the Creek braves under my feet
> and the City of Macon at my back.

This poem, "The Mound Builders," "came out of the resumption of nuclear testing by President Kennedy in 1962 . . . ," Kunitz recalled, and the thought is about the historical and dramatic irony of the epigraph—the self-complimenting and self-satisfied words of the inscription at Ocmulgee National Monument, Georgia, "Macon is the seventh layer of civilization on this spot." "Macon," Kunitz says ironically, "one of the seats of racist injustice in this country."[16]

"Next to Last Things." For the interested reader of Kunitz's work, almost all of the poems in *The Testing-Tree* are startlingly different from those he had written previously. Only a few poems—"Three Floors," "Indian Summer at Land's End," "An Old Cracked Tune," and "Again! Again!"—are at all like the Kunitz of *Selected Poems*. Here instead poems "ruthlessly" examine past injuries, present guilt in dashingly free forms in tones that range from the utmost tenderness to an unpitying savage irony. Three poems from three different sections of *The Testing-Tree* can epitomize the vision in this book, "Around Pastor Bonhoeffer," "The Mulch," and, finally, "The Testing-Tree," the title poem itself.

The three parts of "Around Pastor Bonhoeffer" present in three vignettes the significance of the "German Lutheran pastor and theologian whose Christian conscience forced him, against the pacific temper of his spirit, to accept the necessity of political activism and to join in a conspiracy for the murder of Hitler" (TT, 65). The use of "Around" in the title of the sequence instead of the more conventional "To" or "For" or "About" seems to mean that these are thoughts circling *around* Bonhoeffer, the Bonhoeffer experience, not necessarily thoughts getting to the center of his significance. The first poem, "The Plot Against Hitler," shows the Bonhoeffer family "rehearsing a cantata/for Papa's seventy-fifth birthday" (TT, 12). The contrasts between the scene—family, music, a ceremonial occasion—and what has been planned, the murder of Hitler, are clear. The longest line is "Surely the men had arrived at their stations." And the two lines which end the poem, "*Lord, let the phone ring!/Let the phone ring!"* are Bonhoeffer's prayer that the call will come to say that the plot had succeeded. It did not.

The title of the second poem, "Next to Last Things," alludes to the eschatological "last things" and gives Bonhoeffer's thoughts and justifications, the why of his joining in the plot against Hitler, first in lines of fragmentary near invective:

> Slime, in the grains of the State,
> like smut in the corn,
> from the top infected.
> Hatred made law,
> wolves bred out of maggots
> rolling in blood,
> and the seal of the church ravished
> to receive the crooked sign.

Bonhoeffer's own thoughts in italics come near the center of the poem: *"if you permit/this evil, what is the good/of the good of your life?"* The balancing of "evil" and "good" in the middle of these two and a half lines points up the problem.

> And he forsook the last things,
> the dear inviolable mysteries—
> Plato's lamp, passed from the hand
> of saint to saint—
> that he might risk his soul in the streets,
> where the things given
> are only next to last. . . .

The third poem in the sequence draws away from Bonhoeffer to view him through the eyes of the doctor at the extermination camp where Bonhoeffer was executed: "I was most deeply moved by the way/this lovable man prayed,/so devout and so certain/that God heard his prayer." Then in the last lines of this third poem Bonhoeffer goes to be hanged by the Nazis at Flössenburg before he was forty:

> Round-faced, bespectacled, mild,
> candid with costly grace,
> he walked toward the gallows
> and did not falter.
> Oh but he knew the Hangman!
> Only a few steps more
> and he would enter the arcanum
> where the Master
> would take him by the shoulder,
> as He does at each encounter,
> and turn him round
> to face his brothers in the world.

These last lines of "Around Pastor Bonhoeffer" have about them, as
Stanley Moss has said, "something Talmudic.... Basic to the
Jewish concept of atonement is the position that if you wrong a man,
only he can forgive you, not God." [17] Through these lines gently echo,
too, the final "-er" syllables of "falter," "enter," "shoulder," "encounter," and "brothers," and, as well, "Round-faced" at the
beginning of the passage and "round" near the end, to make a muted
music.

Besides all this, "Some of the details" of the sequence, as Kunitz
noted, "have their source in Bonhoeffer's two posthumous publica-
tions, *The Cost of Discipleship* and *Letters and Papers from Prison*,
and in the biography of his disciple Eberhard Bethge" (TT, 65). The
phrase "costly grace," for instance, is from a distinction Bonhoeffer
makes in *The Cost of Discipleship*—that between "cheap" and
"costly grace": "Costly grace is the gospel which must be *sought* again
and again, the gift which must be *asked* for, the door at which a man
must knock." [18] "Next to last things" and "last things," too, are
Bonhoeffer terms, "penultimate" and "ultimate." [19] The account of
the Bonhoeffer family rehearsing a cantata and the camp doctor's
words about his own reaction to Bonhoeffer's kneeling to pray ("'I
was most deeply moved . . .'") are both from Bethge's biography, the
latter an exact quotation. [20]

Totaling a mere sixty-six lines altogether, most of them short, the
three poems of the sequence are a stunning performance, and perhaps
nowhere in *The Testing-Tree* is the free verse better than in the final
seven lines beginning "Only a few steps more . . ." (quoted above). At
the same time, like other lines such as those after "dear inviolable
mysteries," these lines convey Bonhoeffer's faith and the Bonhoeffer
experience even to those who might not know the story, and so make
"Around Pastor Bonhoeffer" a deeply moving, religious poetic
sequence.

Like other poems in *The Testing-Tree*—"King of the River,"
"River Road"—both "The Mulch" and "The Testing-Tree" lift life
into ritual. Nothing so simple as a "nature" poem "The Mulch"
shows, rather, that man and poet are, as Stanley Moss has said, "a
mulch, a protector locked into nature." [21] The twenty-one lines of this
poem (TT, 21) begin with an action: a man watches a gull trying to
break open a piss-clam. The man himself is gathering salt hay to
mulch his garden, for, as he thinks in one of the two quotations in the
poem, "It is a blue and northern air . . . ," time to protect his garden
against the winter. The mysterious quality of the poem is attained

through almost legendary, repetitive actions: like the gull the man too must "Repeat. Repeat." Each year he must gather "salt hay/in bushel baskets crammed to his chin. . . ." The use of the third person and such lines as "A man with a leaf in his head," "everywhere he goes he carries/a bag of earth on his back," "his heart is an educated swamp," make the actions in the poem archetypal and, indeed, subtly allegorical, saying something about the human condition as well as about caring for a garden. As Kunitz said, although "gardening is a very deep, intimate part" of his poetic life, he is "not tempted to write conventional garden poems. That's too obvious." [22] The meaning and magic in "The Mulch" are not "obvious" on first readings.

In "The Testing-Tree" (TT, 60–63), finally, the subject is an archetypal game the young protagonist plays on his way home from school. From a symbolical "fifty measured paces" he hurls "perfect stones" at an "inexhaustible oak." This "stone-throwing," Kunitz says in his note,

was of a somewhat special order, since it did more than try my skill: it challenged destiny. My life hinged on the three throws permitted me, according to my rules. If I hit the target-oak once, somebody would love me; if I hit it twice, I should be a poet; if I scored all three times, I should never die.

(TT, 67)

This game, Kunitz adds, "is recognizable as an ancient ritual . . . the patriarchal scarred oak . . . is transparently a manifestation of the King of the Wood." [23] And of course the three throws of the game are also the mystical three of myth and ritual like three wishes or three gifts, here those of love, vocation, and immortality. The poem itself is in patterns of three, the lines triads of successively indented lines, and the game-playing part of the poem in only the first three of the four numbered parts.

The fourth section, eleven triads or thirty-three lines, in archetypal terms plays over the journey of life in the disguise of a strange "recurring dream" that seems to arrange life in another tripartite pattern of youth, maturity, and old age: the persona's mother here is a bride, and there are meaningful dream images of a doorway, a well, "an albino walrus," and "dirt [that] keeps sifting in,/staining the water yellow. . . ." One object is displaced by another as the "Model A" unfurls "a highway behind/where the tanks maneuver. . . ."

After the account of this strange dream, the poet leaves that surreal world and makes two wise generalizations, summing up life, guilt, and possibly the archetypal meaning of all this:

In a murderous time
the heart breaks and breaks
and lives by breaking.
It is necessary to go
through dark and deeper dark
and not to turn.

In the first of these two beautifully arranged triads, one "break," the
end of the line, comes after the second "breaks," the word, and then
the next line "breaks" (ends) after the descending rhythm of
"breaking" (the third sound of "break" in the two lines). In the other
triad ("It is necessary . . .") the syntactic and consonant patterns of
the first and third lines ("*necessary to go*," "*not to turn*") are played
off against the dark d's of the second line. The last three lines of the
poem, three successively shorter sentences (7, 6, and 5 syllables),
move from statement to question to an exclamatory cry:

I am looking for the trail.
Where is my testing-tree?
Give me back my stones!

It is a desolate "message" like the one in the first poem in the book,
"Journal for My Daughter," "*What do I want of my life?/More!
More!*"

II   The Terrible Threshold *(1974)*

Poems from Kunitz's first book, *Intellectual Things*, are excluded
from his fifth book, *The Terrible Threshold: Selected Poems,
1940–1970*. The three sections of the book instead coincide with
Kunitz's other three volumes of poetry so that the overall design is
primarily chronological. The seventy-nine poems are arranged in
these numbered and titled parts: I, "The Tumbling of a Leaf," twenty
poems from *Passport to the War* and one from *Selected Poems*;[24] II,
"This Garland, Danger," thirty-two poems from *Selected Poems*; and
III, "Next to Last Things," twenty-six poems from *The Testing-Tree*.
The ordering of the poems is entirely new, with some important
poems from *Passport to the War* omitted from the first section—for
instance, "My Surgeons," "Night Letter," and "The Fitting of the
Mask."[25] Four of the translations in *The Testing-Tree* are omitted
from section 3.[26] Unfortunately *The Terrible Threshold* is available
only in England, for it is quite well worth examining for what the

differing arrangements tell about how Kunitz regards the poems looking at them anew in the 1970s.

As in *Selected Poems* each section title, thematic, is from a poem in that part. "The Tumbling of a Leaf" is from "The Harsh Judgment" (p. 12), a 1941 sonnetlike poem of two seven-line stanzas about a separation at the end of a love. The protagonist wants "Not to be tender-minded . . . ," and to himself as well as to his former beloved he cries, "Courage! That pity made our hearts unclean." The titular phrase comes in line 11, "Last night, last year, with the tumbling of a leaf,/ The autumn came." The repetition of "Last" in the opening of the line linking "night" and "year" clearly makes this more than a seasonal change. "The Harsh Judgment" is the necessity for the action to be taken, and "the tumbling of a leaf" thematically would be the portentousness of such small incidents in life. Sorrow, regret, pity, "The burden of the personal" (p. 12), "The enemies of life" (p. 16), a remembering of "the end of love" (p. 11), of "crimes/ Against us" (p. 13), of "the heart unstrung" (p. 14), a discarding of "That part of your life for which you cared" (p. 15)—these run throughout these early poems, and the section ends with the poem from which the title of the volume comes, "Open the Gates" in which the "I" stands "on the terrible threshold, and . . . see[s]/ The end and the beginning in each other's arms" (p. 22).

The second section title, "This Garland, Danger," is from "Green Ways" (p. 26), a three-stanzaed balladelike poem from the early 1950s, the second poem in *Selected Poems*. Seven times the refrain is negative: "Let me not" or "let me leave untold"—"not say," "not confess," "not reveal." The eighth and ninth times it is "let me but endure" and "Let me proclaim it. . . ." The proclamation is "human be my lot!" The "greennesses" in the poem ("rose-green," "emerald," "green-celled," "green horse-bones") affirm, as Kunitz said, the "I's" "vegetable and mineral existence, as well as his animal self." [27] So it is from his "pit of green horse-bones" that he turns,

> . . . in a wilderness of sweat,
> To the moon-breasted sibylline,
> And lift this garland, Danger, from her throat
> To blaze it in the foundries of the night.

He has not only to accept all parts of himself "in the fullness of the life-process," [28] as Kunitz comments; but he has, indeed, to flaunt them, take the necessary risks. In Kunitz's view the poet "can be a monster. But ideally he is the last representative free man, in that he is beholden to nobody but himself and his own vision of truth." [29] So, in the words from "Welcome the Wrath," he will "not: warp my vision/To square with odds; not scrape; not scamp my fiber ..." (p. 14; SP, 81).

The third and last section of *The Terrible Threshold*, "Next to Last Things," derives its title from that of the second poem in the Bonhoeffer sequence and is Bonhoeffer's own phrase to describe his choice of risking "his soul in the streets,/where the things given/are only next to last;/in God's name cheating, pretending,/playing the double agent ..." (p. 71; TT, 13). This title, "Next to Last Things," is more descriptive of these poems from *The Testing-Tree* than the book title itself, for, as commented on above, in these poems of his sixties Kunitz reviews his life, his mistakes, his failures, his betrayals as a penultimate estimate of the universe. The arrangement of the poems in section 2 of *The Terrible Threshold*, except for omissions, followed that in *Selected Poems*; in this section, aside from ending with the same two poems as in *The Testing-Tree*, the poems have been redistributed again. The poem in the middle of the group is "The Artist" (pp. 77–78), about Mark Rothko, "a dear friend" of Kunitz's.[30] Surrealistic in the beginning, Rothko's paintings increasingly were large, darkly colored rectangles, "tall scenery," in Kunitz's phrase. "The Four Seasons" wall panels for a restaurant, now displayed in a room of their own in the Tate Gallery in London, are in depressingly dark shades of maroon and black, and yet are not Rothko's bleakest and not, literally, his blackest paintings.

In an interview Kunitz commented that he remembered telling Rothko once "that every genius is a monster." "The adversary artist in our time pays a price, in human terms, for his excess of ego and sensibility," Kunitz went on to say to the interviewer:

He has had to sacrifice too much; he is poisoned by ambition; and he carries too big a load of griefs and shames. . . . You're not likely to find him open, generous, or joyous. Rothko, incidentally, killed himself by slashing his wrists not long after our discussion.[31]

In "The Artist" Kunitz presents the artist as "trapped in his monumental void,/raving against his adversaries" (p. 77).

At last he took a knife in his hand
and slashed an exit for himself
between the frames of his tall scenery.
Through the holes cf his tattered universe
the first innocence and the light
came pouring in.

When the "next to last things" cannot satisfy, death is the escape.

CHAPTER 6

"In the Language That We Love":
Translations

C AN poetry be translated? "Poets are the first to concede that the
translation of poetry is an impossibility," Kunitz himself wrote
in 1961; "but," he added, "the knowledge does not deter them from
the effort."[1] A few years later he elaborated on this second point:
"While academicians insist that poetry is untranslatable, poets
continue to produce their translations—never in greater proliferation
or diversity than now."[2]

Through the years more than once Kunitz has "Englished" poems
from other languages: from Spanish and Italian; from the French
(Baudelaire's "To the Reader" in *Selected Poems*); and, most
importantly, from the Russian—poems by Yevtushenko, Voznesensky, Mandelstam, and Akhmatova. In 1974 he published a
translation of Voznesensky's dramatic poem *Story under Full Sail* as
a separate volume; the translations on which Kunitz "worked,"
however, "in close collaboration for several years" with the Oxford
scholar and linguist Max Hayward are those of Anna Akhmatova,
and these significant translations are the principal subject of this
chapter.

What are Kunitz's translations like? What is their value? Also what
"affinity" (Kunitz's word[3]) might they have to his work such as
to make translation his main occupation over several years? Finally,
what is Kunitz's own theory of translation? Space and my general
purpose do not permit lengthy answers to these questions, and so I
shall merely touch upon each of them as I briefly discuss the
translations Kunitz included in *The Testing-Tree* and, as well, that of
the Voznesensky dramatic poem, and then, at somewhat more
leisure, supply some further answers as I examine his versions of
Akhmatova's poems, especially "Poem Without a Hero."

I *Translations in* The Testing-Tree

The six poems from Russian among the thirty in *The Testing-Tree* vary considerably in theme and form. "Summer Solstice/—*from Osip Mandelstam*," as an example, is a comparison between a sense of the slowness of time in the season of summer and the mechanics of verse. The first of the two quatrains ends,

> Once and once only a year nature knows quantity
> stretched to the limit, as in Homer's meter. (TT, 25)

The Mandelstam poem that follows is entitled "Tristia"; the "Latin . . . , meaning Poems of Sorrow, alludes to the elegaic epistles of Ovid," Kunitz writes in his "Notes," "which the Roman poet began on his journey into exile in Tomis. Ovid spoke of the sorrow of exile, of his unconquerable will to survive and to write, of his loves, and of his hope that he might be allowed to return to Rome. Mandelstam," Kunitz concludes, "never returned from the prison camp to which Stalin sent him" (TT, 65). So Mandelstam's farewells in this poem are final farewells; several are catalogued, especially that between man and woman. The last of the four eight-lined stanzas ends by making a contrast between the fates of men and those of women:

> Wax is for women what bronze is for men.
> We, who move blindly toward a world of shades,
> only in battle dare confront our fate,—
> but their gift is to die while telling fortunes. (TT, 27)

Yevtushenko's "Hand-Rolled Cigarettes," in section 3 with other political poems, rings witty changes on the Russian practice of "rolling tobacco in *Pravda* or *Isvestia*, the two top official newspapers" (TT, 66). These nine quatrains, rhymed xaxa, make a serious joke of the glowing fire of burning tobacco eating "up the newsprint, line by line." The poem ends enigmatically with

> Listen! they roll another cigarette:
> and history is on their side. (TT, 39)

Like some of the other poems in this section of *The Testing-Tree*, this one has a light-hearted surface and tone which make more bitter the content.

The Aba Stolzenberg poem "Bolsheviks," translated from Yiddish, encapsulates a historical moment and makes a contrast between the childlike, unprepared Bolsheviks and the efficient White Guards. Possibly to mirror the disorder of the time, each of the three stanzas has a different rhyme pattern: in the first, "bullets" and "leaders" of lines two and three share an "s" sound; "packs" and "sacks" of lines four and five (and last in the stanza) rhyme exactly. In the two remaining stanzas, quatrains, one rhymes xaxa, with "a" an exact rhyme, "hand-land"; the other, abab, off-rhyme, "where-here," "Guards-woods" (TT, 44).

Of the three translations of Anna Akhmatova that open part IV of *The Testing-Tree*, the first, "Boris Pasternak," her tribute to her great peer and friend, is almost a quintessential "artist" poem, what the artist does in vivid image after image, what "it means," and how he is "rewarded." The artist's eye alters what it observes so that it is never the same again: "puddles shine, ice grieves and liquefies." Stanza three begins with sound ("ringing, roaring, grinding, breakers' crash . . .") followed by silence, the turn in the poem:

> and silence all at once, release;
> it means he is tiptoeing over pine needles,
> so as not to startle the light sleep of space.
>
> And it means he is counting the grains
> in the blasted ears; it means
> he has come again to the Daryal Wall,
> accursed and black, from another funeral.
>
> And again Moscow, where the heart's fever burns;
> far off the deadly sleighbell chimes;
> someone is lost two steps from home
> in waist-high snow. The worst of times. . .[4]

These lines from the middle of the poem include several of its strong effects—the allusiveness, the effective imagery, the subtle rhyme. The last two quoted lines, for instance, can almost stand for the real horror under the everyday surface of the Russian life that Pasternak and Akhmatova knew. To be lost a mere "two steps from home" justifies the fragmentary "The worst of times . . ."—the dots of the ellipsis are in Kunitz's text—because no "best of times" is possible.

The main pattern of rhyme through the seven quatrains is xaxa, but it is altered in the fourth, sixth, and seventh stanzas. The fourth stanza (quoted above, "And it means . . .") rhymes aabb; Kunitz changed "Wall" to "Gorge" before including the poem in his Akhmatova volume, not, he said, to avoid the rhyme, but to be more exact. With end-words "grains-means" and "Gorge-funeral," the stanza, however, in revision is like the others in the poem, one pair of rhymes a quatrain.

Akhmatova's "Dante" concerns this poet and his "beloved Florence," and is a poem of exile and the exile's love of home.

> Even after his death he did not return
> to the city that nursed him.
> Going away, this man did not look back.
> To him I sing this song.   (TT, 53)

The next four lines in two sentences give the situation in Florence and Dante's attachment to his native city:

> Torches, night, a last embrace,
> outside in her streets the mob howling.
> He sent her a curse from hell
> and in heaven could not forget her.

The turn comes in the ninth line with "But":

> But never, in a penitent's shirt,
> did he walk barefoot with lighted candle
> through his beloved Florence,
> perfidious, base, and irremediably home.

The final modifiers of Florence—"perfidious, base, and irremediably home"—bear the weight of the poet's meaning. The date of Akhmatova's poem, 1936, is a year in the time of her "inner emigration," or exile at home. During the difficult time for writers in Russia, Akhmatova, like many of her fellows, "retired," as one of her biographers says, "entirely from life, although she continued to write." In the early 1920s and later "she found refuge in scholarship."[5] Biographically, "Dante" may be an explanation of an "inner émigré's" feelings.

The twelve undivided lines of "Dante," quoted in full above, are sonnetlike in form, the "But" beginning what would be the sestet of a sonnet. The twelve lines of "Cleopatra" are divided into three quatrains: one delineates the situation; the second gives present action; the third and last pictures the future:

>   Nothing
> remains except to tease this fellow out of mind
> and put the black snake, like a parting act of pity,
> on her dark breast with indifferent hand.   (TT, 54)

The alliteration of the "p's" and "b's" and the assonance of "parting" and "dark" uncoil the last two lines so that the emphasis falls on the final phrase, especially on "indifferent," to suggest the stoic courage and dignity of Cleopatra's last moments.

Until Kunitz corrected me on this, I regarded the Korzhavin lines entitled by him "The Bottom of the Glass" as a translation and said about them that here alone of the "translations" was a poem akin to Kunitz's own. Since it is an "imitation" and thus his own poem, I have to say that the translations seem to me, on the whole, less subjective than Kunitz usually is, more "occasional," too, and, at times, more austere.

II   *Voznesensky's* Story Under Full Sail

In answer to Andrei Voznesensky's request that his dramatic poem *Story Under Full Sail* be translated, in 1971 a group of Slavists, Vera Reck, Maureen Sager, and Catherine Leach, undertook a literal English version and also annotated the text and supplied a Historical Note. Kunitz, then, is responsible for translating what they had done into verse, most likely an act of friendship to make available in the United States a bilingual edition of this poem by his friend the contemporary Russian poet.[6]

Story Under Full Sail itself is made up of ten parts and a preface, mostly short, lyrical, and, sometimes, satirical sections, dramatizing a story from the American and Russian past. The historical tale concerns a love between an aristocratic Russian from Catherine the Great's court, Rezanov, and Concha Arguello, the sixteen-year-old daughter of the Spanish commandant of the San Francisco presidio. These strange conjunctions of people and place were brought about by Russian expansion in the North Pacific in the nineteenth century. After they were betrothed Rezanov was called away by his duties; he died; years later, when she heard the news, Concha became a nun. Rezanov and Concha's romantic story has interested others— California writers Bret Harte and Gertrude Atherton are two who have also told the story—and Voznesensky's retelling of the sequence has some interest, but not, I think, any great dramatic force.

III *Poems of Akhmatova*

"Pasternak," "Dante," and "Cleopatra," all three of the Akhmatova translations in *The Testing-Tree*, are included in Kunitz's Akhmatova volume of 1973, and, in addition, thirty-seven other poems, arranged, as Kunitz says, given her career, "The only way" possible, "chronologically." Sixteen of these forty are from the decade 1909–1919; four from the 1920s; nine from the 1930s; five from the 1940s; and five from 1960 and 1961. The important last one, "Poem without a Hero," written in the 1940s, Akhmatova kept returning to and revising, and thus it is a 1950s poem, too, partly filling in that decade in which she is otherwise silent in this volume. Not one of these forty poems was "selected for inclusion," Kunitz wrote, "that was not judged conspicuously fine or representative, either in the body of the work as a whole, or with reference to a specific category, such as the love poems or the 'patriotic verse' of World War I."[7]

The book itself, 173 pages long, is made up of 1) Max Hayward's twenty-four-page introduction; 2) a short "Note on the Translations" by Kunitz; 3) translations of forty of Akhmatova's poems with facing Russian texts; and 4) a few pages of "Notes on the Poems." The first thing that must be said, then, is that the scant number of poems, forty out of Akhmatova's approximately 800, of course makes this a "selection" of her work. To make a numerical analogy it would be as if of Kunitz's total work we read only one-twentieth, say, five or so of his poems.

That said, these forty poems are, nonetheless, a fine selection, including as they do some of Akhmatova's best poems—"Lot's Wife," for example, and "Dante," "Requiem," "The Death of Sophocles," and a section from her long, complicated, important "Poem without a Hero." What are these poems like? Most of them are short, eight to twelve lines, sometimes twenty lines long; like "Pasternak" a few are longer, twenty-eight or twenty-nine lines. Only two sequences, "Requiem" and "In 1940," combinations of short lyrics, and "Poem without a Hero," a narrative poem, are at all lengthy. As a consequence, many Akhmatova poems are compressed like haikus, intensely sober, sad poems about unhappy and tragic events, persons, and passions. From what I have read in other translations of her poems, these selected by Kunitz accurately reflect her work as a whole.

Page one of the book has Akhmatova's name and dates and two meaningful epigraphs from two of her important poems:

> And over the legendary embankment
> the real, not the calendar
> Twentieth Century drew near.
>
> —"Poem without a Hero,"
> Part I, chapter 3
>
> No foreign sky protected me,
> no stranger's wing shielded my face.
> I stand as witness to the common lot,
> survivor of that time, that place.
>
> —"Requiem"

Time, courage, her own role as witness, exile, love of country, love itself—these are Akhmatova's subjects—given "with no idiosyncrasy of surface or of syntax," clearly, cleanly. "Her poems exist," Kunitz said, "in the purity and exactness of their diction, the authority of their tone, the subtlety of their rhythmic modulations, the integrity of their form."[8]

For, as Russian poet Joseph Brodsky notes in his review of this book, Akhmatova "is an extremely restrained poet, almost simple. But her simplicity is like the 'simplicity' of Robert Frost. . . ." The "best" Russian poets, Brodsky maintains,

. . . never allow themselves hysterics on paper, pathological confessions, spilling ashes over their heads, curses aimed at the guilty, no matter what the character of the events which they become witness to, participants in, or sometimes, victims of.

In Akhmatova's verse this results, Brodsky says, in a "falling intonation toward the end, as if nothing special has happened."[9]

Thus a poem with a histrionic, even hysterical action in its first line, "I Wrung My Hands . . . ," one of her best known, has a characteristic picture, details, and so a dying fall: The wringing of the hands and the "dark veil," feminine action and costume; the question and explanation; then the dip into the past to dramatize the emotional scene; and, finally, an understated exchange of dialogue in the last stanza. The persona shouts,

> . . . choking: "I meant it all
> in fun. Don't leave me, or I'll die of pain."
> He smiled at me—oh so calmly, terribly—
> and said: "Why don't you get out of the rain?"   (43)

"This Cruel Age Has Deflected Me . . ." similarly begins on a high emotional note and falls off. "Deflected" her "changeling life has flowed/into a sister channel." She has "Missed" much—"spectacles," "friends," "foreign skylines" she has failed to write verses also. Her very self has been "usurped."

> The grave I go to will not be my own.
> But if I could step outside myself
> and contemplate the person that I am,
> I should know at last what envy is.   (129–31)

Like the river simile in this poem—"This cruel age has deflected me,/like a river from its course."—some images and phrases in Ahkmatova's poetry stand out: "your eyes like a cautious cat," "bonfires of roses in the snow," "Fingered the foulest wounds," "Death's great black wing," "wormwood infects your foreign bread," "a paperweight of trees, walls, snow." These are Akhmatova's own, we know, because they appear in other translations. The first one, for example, has also been rendered, "Like the eyes of a cautious cat . . ."; the second, "crimson bonfires/like roses flower in the snow." [10]

"Poem without a Hero." Of "Poem without a Hero" only part of "the first chapter of the poem's Part One," about a third of the poem, is translated by Kunitz and Hayward. This poem, written in 1940–1943, "continued to preoccupy [Akhmatova] long after its completion . . . ," Max Hayward writes, "becoming something of an obsession." [11] Though she had "completely stopped writing poetry," Akhamatova explained in 1955 in "A Letter to N.,"

. . . still for fifteen years this poem kept catching me unexpectedly, over and over, like fits of some incurable disease (it could happen anywhere—at concerts to the music, on the street, even in my dreams), and I could not tear loose from it, as I kept adding to and correcting an apparently completed work. [12]

For the full title of "Poem without a Hero" one has to go to the "Notes": "The Year Nineteen Hundred and Thirteen: A Petersburg Tale"; also omitted in this translation are "the preface and three dedications in verse . . ." (166). Most of this no doubt is better not included; it would have been a confusing, fussy introduction for this excerpt. For further information about the fragment itself, the reader

of the Akhmatova volume can go to Hayward's introduction and the
"Notes" at the end to find out that "Poem" is a narrative poem, a
novel in verse, something like Pushkin's "Bronze Horseman." A more
familiar comparison might be Pushkin's *Eugene Onegin*, a narrative
poem sometimes called "the first Russian novel," or Byron's *Don
Juan*, from which one of Akhmatova's epigraphs comes.

The subtitle of part I of "Poem without a Hero," "A Petersburg
Tale," points to the importance of its genre; like Pushkin's "Bronze
Horseman," which is also "A Petersburg Tale," Akhmatova's poem
will frame its central characters in history. And, as the "Notes" say,
Akhmatova regarded this long poem of hers "as the crowning work of
her life, a final distillation of memory, historical insight, and personal
emotion into a poetic statement about the destiny of Russia" (168).
To do all this she handles such romantic themes as memories of
one's younger days, an old love, poetry, death, and deals with such
Russian literary figures as, first of all, Vsevolod Knyazev, and, also,
Osip Mandelstam, Olga Glebova-Sudeikina, Alexander Blok, and
others.

Chapter 1 itself is set specifically in time, "New Year's Eve," 1940,
and in place, "A white hall of mirrors" in "The House on the
Fontanka [Canal]," St. Petersburg. Alone "on this ceremonial eve" of
the turn of the year, the author "is visited by shadows from the year
1913 disguised as mummers." Immediately preceding the opening
year of World War I, 1913 for everyone is the final year of the old way
of life; for the author this date twenty-seven years before is personally
important, also, as the year when her friend the young poet Vsevolod
Knyazev committed suicide.

When "The insistent doorbell rings," she says

> ... in a far-off voice:
> "You've come to the wrong place,
> the Doges' Palace is next door,
> but welcome! Leave in the hall
> your masks, cloaks, scepters, crowns.
> My pleasure is to celebrate you now,
> New Year's revelers!"   (147)

The mummers come in as Faust, Don Juan, John the Baptist, Dorian
Gray, and others including the Prince of Darkness himself, to a total
of seven. Halfway through the excerpt are premonitions of an eighth
visitor:

> *All the mirrors on the wall*
> *show a man not yet appeared*
> *who could not enter this white hall.*[13]

Mirrors which reflect someone not present are a typical detail in the dreamlike happenings of the poem. Some fifty lines later this eighth figure is referred to again:

> A shout:
> "Make way for the hero!"
> Ah yes. Displacing the tall one,
> he will step forth now without fail
> and sing to us about holy vengeance . . .
>
> (153; ellipsis in text)

The verb, though, is the future tense—"will step forth"—for he does not appear. This is a poem "without a hero" because Akhmatova's

main purpose was to recall an era in which there were no heroes, only pseudo-Romantic masqueraders; the hero-individualist of the nineteenth century had come to the end of the road and his epigones (unless, like Knyazev, they died young) would be offered up wholesale to the Moloch of war and revolution. (167)

As the "Notes" add, "The 'real, not the calendar Twentieth Century' had no need of heroes."

The author then questions why the mummers are

> . . . all running away,
> as if each of you had found a bride,
> leaving me face to face
> in the gloom with a black picture-frame,
> out of which stares that very hour,
> prologue to the bitterest drama of my life,
> which I have yet to expiate. (153)

As in many of Akhmatova's poems, in "Poem without a Hero" the persona here returns to an episode of an ill-starred love as a climactic moment in life. Kynazev, the eighth visitor who never appears, had killed himself after seeing the woman he loved come home with someone else, quite an unheroic happening.

The visitation here ends with a "*Goodbye,*" whispered by an unidentified "*him,*" presumably Knyazev.

> *"I shall leave you behind* [he adds].
> *but you will be my widow.*
> *O my dove, my star, my sister!"*
> *On the landing two locked shadows . . .*
> *then the broad steps plunge beneath.*
> *"Don't do it!" In the distance*
> *a pure voice: "I am ready for death."*
>   (155; italics and ellipsis in text)

The prose passage that follows restores order with stage directions:
"The torches go out, the ceiling drops into place. The white hall of
mirrors becomes the author's room. Words from the darkness. . . ."
These final words are quiet, non-explanatory:

> There is no death, each of us knows—
> it's banal to say.
> I'll leave it to others to explain.
> That knocking!
>   I thought all of them were here.
> Is this the visitor from the wrong side
>   of the mirror? Or the shape
> that suddenly flitted past my window?
> Is it the new moon playing tricks,
> or is someone really standing there again
> between the stove and the cupboard?
> Pale forehead. Open eyes . . .
> This means that gravestones are fragile
> and granite is softer than wax.
> Absurd, absurd, absurd! From such absurdity
> I shall soon turn gray
> or change into another person.
> Why do you beckon me with your hand?
>
>> *For one moment of peace*
>> *I would give the peace of the tomb.*
>   (155; italics and ellipsis in text)

Since it is not included in the Kunitz-Hayward translation, the
rest of "Poem without a Hero" need not concern us here. The "Notes"
supply a discriminating summary of the remainder, though, with
extensive quotations from various parts. Chapter 2, for example, is
said to open "with a kind of scherzo in which there is a conversation
with an imaginary editor in the Soviet present. He is disconcerted by
the confusion in Part One: 'You can't make out who's dead and who

survived,/who the author is and who the hero,/or why today we need such/gossip about a poet and this swarm of ghosts.'" One commentator also says, "Without some explanation of allusions and background, Akhmatova's poem will seem more opaque than it really is."[14]

Point by point so it may be. Yet to a reader of the Kunitz-Hayward volume, who the visitors are biographically does not supremely matter. The visitation itself may seem a little like Kunitz's own "phantoms and phobias" of "Night Letter" or the brief, elliptical appearance of Dante in "The Illumination." And like those and others in Kunitz's poems, Akhmatova's shadows, phantoms, ghosts from her past of more than a quarter of a century before have come to torment her, and this is sufficient to know: *"For one moment of peace/I would give the peace of the tomb."*

This fragment by itself is superb, the action and details universalized into a general sense of guilt and doom. As an example the following passage in the middle of this section from the poem typifies Akhmatova's tone, materials, and syntax—"no idiosyncrasy of surface or of syntax . . .":

> But why, among them, must I be
> the only one alive?
> Tomorrow morning I shall wake
> and nobody will accuse me.
> Through the window the bluest sky
> will laugh in my face. But now
> I am afraid. I shall present myself,
> not taking off my lace shawl,
> and manage a vague smile
> before falling silent.
> That woman I once was,
> in a black agate necklace,
> I do not wish to meet again
> till the Day of Judgment.
> Are the last days near, perhaps?
> I have forgotten your lessons,
> prattlers and false prophets,
> but you haven't forgotten me.
> As the future ripens in the past,
> so the past rots in the future—
> a terrible festival of dead leaves.   (149)

This last figure of speech, which one critic finds "central" to "Poem" and suggestive, too, of Akhmatova's later work,[15] is magnificently handled in Kunitz's translation: the vegetative verbs "ripens" and "rots" are linked together by alliteration to convey this mixing of future and past, past and future. Kunitz's accomplishment here can be partially judged by comparing "ripens" and "rots" with "ripens" and "moulder" in another translation, or "ripens" and "decays" in a third version, or with "The future matures in the past whose embers glow in the future" in yet another translation.[16]

IV   *An Assessment of the Akhmatova Translations*

A work as important as Akhmatova's "Poem without a Hero" should naturally be translated in its entirety, as it has been by other hands. The six pages here in the Kunitz-Hayward book, nonetheless, give some hint of the force of the whole poem. The Russian poet Joseph Brodsky, a protégé of Akhmatova's, complained about the form used in this excerpt, yet granted that the volume of translations in itself was "a good book," and "in a clear sense Akhmatova was lucky with her translator. . . ."[17] Michael Mesic has said about these translations, too, that "they are excellent, better than one ever expected them to be. . . ." Still, he continued, "We should . . . accept and appreciate [them] . . . not only as some of the best presently available, but as guides to better."[18]

Akhmatova's poetry has been translated by others besides Kunitz and Hayward: Richard McKane did a *Selected Poems* in 1969; Joseph Langland, Eugene M. Kayden, Jamie Fuller, and Carl R. Proffer have been publishing their versions of some of Akhmatova's poems; Robert Lowell and Olga Carlisle translated "Requiem."[19] All of this is surely no more than the due of the woman who before her death was called the "greatest living Russian poet" and, since then, "the greatest Russian poetess of the twentieth century."[20] One may wince at the depreciating "-ess" suffix in that last quotation and say with Kunitz (in another connection), "I have never in my life used the word 'poetess,' which strikes me as a diminishing term, calculated to introduce a superfluous sexual qualification."[21] In fact, though, "greatest" is there in both quotations, and Kunitz's dedication through several years to the translation and transmission of Akhmatova's work gives the otherwise unaware reader some intimation of the brave, strong spirit, the fearless voice of this enormously gifted poet.

In truth, one cannot read Max Hayward's superb biographical introduction, the translations themselves, or the concluding notes without being stirred by Akhmatova's work and her story and recognizing, too, why an American poet of Kunitz's stature would have devoted so much of his time to bringing Akhmatova's poetry to poetry-lovers who do not read Russian. Her long life itself (1889–1966) has about it a legendary, mythic quality, spanning as it does more than three-quarters of a century of Russian history, distress, and disaster.[22] As Kunitz says in his "Note":

Tragedy did not wither her: it crowned her with majesty. Her life, in Keats's phrase, became "a continual allegory," its strands interwoven with the story of a people. Indeed, her poems can be read in sequence as a twentieth-century Russian chronicle.[23]

For, in both "This Cruel Age Has Deflected Me . . ." and "Poem without a Hero," as the "Notes" say, she

expresses the wonderment of many of her contemporaries at having been born on the threshold of an era which was to witness "spectacles" of such unreality that it was impossible not to brood on the illusoriness of time itself and even the coordinates of one's own identity.[24]

One reviewer of the Kunitz-Hayward book thought an earlier translation of Akhmatova, Richard McKane's *Selected Poems*, "more faithful to the original and more compelling in English . . . , but it unfortunately lack[ed] the Russian text."[25] One considerable virtue of *Poems of Akhmatova* is certainly its facing Russian versions of the poems. In the instance of what Brodsky calls the "special 'Akhmatova stanza'" of "Poem without a Hero," for example, comparing Kunitz's translation with the Russian, one can see that it is faithful to Akhmatova's lines and punctuation, important elements in her stanzaic form. This "Akhmatova stanza," Brodsky maintains, "in its musical density has nothing equal to it in Russian poetry," and he objects to Kunitz's presenting it in "free verse." "Imagine," Brodsky comments, "'The Hollow Men' translated into sonnets or triolets."[26]

Yet Kunitz's "free verse" here is extremely disciplined in line lengths and sounds and actually hardly free verse at all. Akhmatova's stanzas in part I of the Russian are most often rhyming triads with a few other stanzas of from one to twelve lines interspersed: twenty-seven triads, nine four-lined stanzas, and one each of one, two, five, six, seven, eight, ten, and twelve lines. Each stanza is a syntactically complete unit rigorously duplicated in the translation.

But, yes, in the translation the lines of each stanza are not successively indented as they are in the Russian original, and also they do not begin with capitals except at the openings of sentences. Abstention from these printing formalities makes the English look like freer verse than it actually is. The rhyme, too, is not in the English. Yet, as Kunitz remarked in his "Note on the Translations,"

To insist on a universally rigid duplication of metrical and rhyming patterns is arbitrary and pointless, since the effects in any case are not mechanically transferable to another language. Instead of rhyme, our ear is often better pleased by an instrumentation of off-rhyme, assonance, consonance, and other linkages.   (33–34)

Some of these "linkages" are like the one called attention to in the "Notes": "The translation here takes a slight liberty with the original in order to render a phonetic detail by which Akhmatova set such store that she added a special note on it at the end of the 'Poem': 'The three "k's" betray the author's confusion'" (171).

> Clearly it's me
> they seek, cocoon of souls,
> though not my kind. . . .   (149)

Kunitz's translation has the three initial "k" sounds as well as medial and terminal ones in "cocoon" and in "seek." Another published version of these lines has only one "k" sound:

> It's all clear:
> if not to me, to whom then![27]

In justice to Carl R. Proffer, whose lines I have just compared with Kunitz's, he does say that "The English reader will have to accept Akhmatova's mastery of rhythm and rhyme largely on faith, since the translation itself is not a poetic transformation."[28] The Kunitz-Hayward translation is an attempt at just that—a poetic transformation.

That at times "transformation" is not effected is perhaps no more than to be expected when, as one reviewer notes, "the defects are due to those connotations and that verbal music which are not transferable from one language to another, not to the translator's carelessness, ignorance or indifference." The passage Helen Muchnic points to is in the "Dedication" to "Requiem" in which

... the Russian words for "grief," ... "stoop," ... and "mountains," ... all begin with a hard g, and "grief" is identical with "mountains" except for the final vowel, so that when ... Akhmatova wants to say "under such grief, the mountains stoop," she writes *"pered etim gorem gnutsia gorry,"* a line that in its echoing g's, g-o's and r's *(pered, gorem, gorry)* conveys not only the image of crushing weight but the very sound of stifled groans and the sense of mortal agony. ..."[29]

Kunitz's "alliterative m's and s's" in "Such grief might make the mountains stoop," Muchnic adds, "are too soft for the harsh power of Akhmatova's line." Another translator alliterated b's only: "The mountains bend before this grief. ..."[30] And in fairness to Kunitz and all other translators one has to add that languages do not agree in sound patterns; the descending vowels of Kunitz's line are surely as important as his "alliterative m's and s's" and both are better than the battering of the b's in the other translation at conveying "the harsh power of Akhmatova's line." Meaning as well as sound patterns must be respected, and how else is "Vedor, vedor, vedor!—Ot takogo vedora ..." to be translated except something like "Absurd, absurd, absurd! From such absurdity ..." (154 and 155)? Proffer translates the line "Drivel, drivel, drivel!—From drivel like this ... ," omitting the important alteration in meaning from "vedor" to "vedora." These, though, are some of the perils of attempting a "poetic transformation," as Kunitz explains well in his six-page "Note on the Translations" in the Akhmatova volume. Below I shall merely try to outline his main points.

Kunitz's Theory of Translation. In an interview Kunitz readily admitted that his own "knowledge of Russian is rudimentary. Though my parents came from Russia, I am not a Russian linguist or scholar."[31] And in his "Note" he said candidly,

I wish I were a better linguist than I am, but in default of that aptitude I count myself lucky in this partnership [with Max Hayward]. There are plenty of Slavists, but few who can articulate the fine discriminations that mark the language of poetry. (32)

Between them they have, he said, "a reciprocity of trust and confidence, together with a congeniality of temperament" which has made their collaboration fruitful. "On some occasions," Kunitz added, "I have rather boldly rendered a line or a phrase, but always on aesthetic grounds, never because I felt that my information was unreliable" (32).

For, as Kunitz says earlier in his "Note," "The poet as translator lives with a paradox. His work must not read like a translation; conversely, it is not an exercise of the free imagination. One voice enjoins him: 'Respect the text!' The other simultaneously pleads with him: 'Make it new!'" (29). The two quoted phrases, the second one the hallmark of Ezra Pound's approach to translation, suggest what Kunitz aims for—something closer to the original than Pound's loose renderings, intuitive guesses, and "homages" but at the same time something far from a slavish adherence to a "literal" reading. As Kunitz reflects, "the term [literal version] is definitely a misnomer. . . . Translation is a sum of approximations, but not all approximations are equal" (32).

Illustrating with a "conscientious" "literal version" of one of Akhmatova's poems, Kunitz said of it that

the lines are only a shadow of the original text, incapable of producing its singular pleasures. The object is to produce an analogous poem in English out of available signs and sounds, a new poem sprung from the matrix of the old, drenched in memories of its former existence . . . what it said, how it breathed, the inflections of the voice.   (33; ellipsis in the text)

Akhmatova's is a strong enough voice to come through almost any reasonably good translation—at least I have found this to be so in reading and comparing the work of more than half a dozen different translators of her poems. Still, the high quality of Kunitz's versions is evident, I think, in part in the quotations already made from the poems; then, too, reviewers who know Russian, as I do not, have agreed on the excellence of the translations.

Michael Mesic, for example, says "that we might be tempted to consider [them] . . . unsurpassable." [32] And Helen Muchnic, too, finds the "translations . . . faithful enough and on the whole as good as any we have so far," though she contends that they "are not great poems." It would not be difficult, she writes, "to point out other shortcomings [besides the absence of the alliterative hard g's in "Requiem" already commented on]: instances when for the sake of meaning, rhymes are ignored, or conversely, for the sake of rhyme, an emphasis is changed or the terseness of a line is diluted." Still, Muchnic says, "One can do no less than admire [Kunitz's] . . . courage and feel grateful for [his] . . . ardent effort and appreciation." [33]

The harshest of those reviewing these translations, Joseph Brodsky, grants that "Stanley Kunitz turns out to be a person who is spiritually and technically qualified for the task. If he makes mistakes, the mistakes are more in technical details than in conveying the spirit of the poems chosen. And these mistakes," Brodsky adds, "if they do lead the reader astray, at least do not take him in the opposite direction." Brodsky centers his adverse criticism on "Imitation from the Armenian" and the excerpt from "Poem without a Hero"; on the other hand he believes that "Kunitz achieves considerable success in the poem 'Boris Pasternak,' in many passages of 'Requiem' . . . 'Cleopatra,' and other poems." [34]

I would add a final insistence about the dilemma of the translator: a compiler of an anthology of modern Russian poetry who worked closely with his translator has said, "There must be a middle ground between translators' padding and *otsebyatiny* (one's own concoctions) and pursuing the translating ideal with a Tolstoyan stubbornness so that finally common sense is sacrificed to Integrity." As a result of his own work with Merrill Sparks in Englishing a number of Russian poems Vladimir Markov also confesses that he has "regretted many times the fact [that in the past] he [had] blamed in his reviews other translators who could not do justice to all aspects of their originals." [35] Perfect translation, then, may be an impossibility.

In conclusion I must admit that in the recent past I had wished that in these late years of his life Kunitz had worked less on his translations of Akhmatova and others and more on his own poetry; now I am not so sure but that his was the better course. "The undertaking began with a feeling of admiration for Akhmatova," Kunitz wrote in his "Note"; "it ends with a measure of awe" (30). That "measure of awe" is mine now, too, and it is thus no small gift to his readers and admirers and to poetry-lovers in general that this eminent American poet offers in his translations. Kunitz had been "moved to record what [he] heard," in Akhmatova's poetry, "and to try to give it back in the language that we love" (34).

CHAPTER 7

Seedcorn and Windfall: Kunitz's Prose Book

K UNITZ'S one book of prose, *A Kind of Order, A Kind of Folly: Essays and Conversations* (1975), is made up of fifty pieces, some quite long, some brief, some published for the first time, most selected from the published prose of five decades—essays, conversations, reviews, introductions, personal reflections. Mostly these concern poets and poetry; four are about art and artists; some are autobiographical reminiscences; and some are semiphilosophical, aphoristic journal notes ("Seedcorn and Windfall"). The fifty separate items themselves are arranged under eight main headings, each of which points to the main subject of each section, as, for instance, "Four for Roethke," a collection of Kunitz's writings about Theodore Roethke, or "Root Images," about Kunitz's own boyhood.

The book opens with a brief, explanatory "Foreword," admitting the inevitably "random aspect" that such a gathering together as this must have. Yet, too, Kunitz insists on his stubbornness or "the durability of the psyche" through the years. One of his "unshakable convictions," he writes, "has been that poetry is more than a craft, important as the craft may be: it is a vocation, a passionate enterprise, rooted in human sympathies and aspirations."[1] And this is mostly what the book is about—poetry as a high vocation.

A Kind of Order itself contains both reminiscences and theoretical and analytical essays on poetry and art, personal and informative. "Produced over a span of years"—forty-four, by my count—Kunitz's prose in this book has no one describable style. He did no rewriting, he says in his "Foreword," "for the sake of improving or squaring my opinions," but he did try "to eliminate matter that seemed peripheral to the main thrust of this volume, or patently ephemeral, or boring, or redundant" (xii). Having made comparisons, I can testify that this is indeed fully true. Some passages have been altered to excise details that "date" the writing, others to banish a cliché, something already used elsewhere, or the obvious ("The publication of *The Letters of Wallace Stevens* is an event in American literary history.").

No extensive rewriting was undertaken, however—rightly, I think, for how could one, one might ask in a Kunitzian question, reenvision such random writings as these? What I take to be the latest pieces— "A Kind of Order" and "Seedcorn and Windfall"—have a mature, bright rightness of language, simple elegance of syntax, and aphoristic splendor. The earliest pieces—"The Vaudeville of the Mind (Conrad Aiken)" and "A Lesson from Rilke," two from among more than two dozen reviews and essays of Kunitz's early years—date from his middle and late twenties and are abstruse and rather showy in style. Hence Kunitz's prose changed in a way similar to his poetry. As he noted in "Seedcorn and Windfall," his "early writing was dense and involuted—so, I guess, was I." Now what he seeks "is a transparency of language and vision" (301). At least two pieces, the first and the last (just named above), achieve this "transparency of language and vision"; others similarly have an easygoing, colloquial swing—for instance, the autobiographical essays in "Root Images." But Kunitz's medium is verse, not prose, and one reads *A Kind of Order* for *what* it is saying, not *how*. That is not to say that the book is ill-written, for it assuredly is not. Mainly, though, what the reader gets is lucidity of *thought* and, generally, great good sense. "It is no doubt a judgment of our age," one reviewer wrote, "that we find good sense astounding. Mr. Kunitz has it, and to an astonishing degree. He says a great many things which, in this late frantic hour of our art, need desperately once again to be said—which is to say of course that they need desperately once again to be heard."[2] Even more important, "Romantic notions of the poet notwithstanding," this reviewer, Richard Vine, adds, "poetic sensibility manifestly does not preclude precision of thought; one can be a good poet *and* an accurate thinker. Stanley Kunitz is both."[3]

Outstanding items in the book are Kunitz's portraits of his friends Theodore Roethke and Robert Lowell. Part II brings together four pieces on Roethke written between 1949 and 1965, expert analyses and pertinent personal estimates. The "Conversation" with Robert Lowell, in which only Lowell speaks, has important statements on poetry ranging from Lowell's opinions about other poets to remarks about his own poetry.

Another notable characteristic of *A Kind of Order* is the great number of quotations that it contains. As Kunitz acknowledges in his

"Foreword," "A writer's obsessions and quotations are the indispensable baggage he carries with him from year to year and from page to page," and so obsessive, favorite quotations occur more than once; to "expunge" them, as Kunitz says, would leave "too big a hole in the text" (xii). Each section and each essay begin with quotations; the first section, for example, with quotations from Osip Mandelstam and Herbert Marcuse; the first essay, Siegfried Giedion. Quoted or alluded to in the first essay are Nietzsche, Kierkegaard, Freud, Pascal, Heisenberg, Niels Bohr, Yeats, Einstein, Carlyle, Stevens, Franz Kline, Valéry, Emerson, Lionel Johnson, Pope, Plato, and Tillich. Some others in other essays are Camus, Rilke, Malraux, Whitman, Goethe, Pound, Ortega y Gasset, Serge Diaghilev, Solzhenitsyn, Voznesensky, Belinsky, Yevtushenko, Akhmatova, Joseph Brodsky, Shakespeare, Pasternak, Keats, William Carlos Williams, Confucius, Christopher Caudwell, Whitehead, Chekhov, Blake, Hopkins, Coleridge, Brecht, Fanon, Wordsworth, Joyce, Thomas Mann, Roethke, Lévi-Strauss, Shelley, Frost, Sartre, Lao-Tzu, St. John of the Cross, Dr. Rollo May, and many others—to a total number of about 100 writers, painters, sculptors, and composers. A mind reveals itself by whom and what it remembers, and in his quotations and allusions Kunitz shows himself to be widely read, liberal, humanitarian, reflective—and consistent, in the best sense. Richard Vine, for instance, observes "a uniform quality of mind [that] pervades" the book and adds that it is "a quality marked by reasonableness, sensitivity, lucidity, and balance. One thinks inevitably of Aristotle's Magnanimous Man, of Camus' *homme du midi*."[4] So here Stanley Kunitz's highly individual voice is echoed and counterpointed by those of others to create a polyphony of thought, one of the more admirable aspects of *A Kind of Order, A Kind of Folly.*

I *The Style of an Age*

At the end of his "Foreword" Kunitz plays on Yeats's words by saying that "In the medium of prose a poet walks more naked than in his verse" (xii), and so here in the first section one sees Kunitz's ideas plain. The first long essay, "A Kind of Order," is one of six on "The Style of an Age," part I of the book, and like "Seedcorn and Windfall," the essay that makes up part VIII and ends the book, it is a major expression of Kunitz's thoughts on poets and poetry. Though less so than "Seedcorn," "A Kind of Order" still tends to be an essay in the Emersonian tradition of bits of journal jottings stitched into a single whole. In other words, it shines with flashes of insight pithily stated. Still, some paragraphs remain under- or undeveloped and its main idea—the necessity of balancing inner and outer realities, as pointed to in the Giedion epigraph*—is more outlined than analyzed. Yet, overall, as might be expected, "A Kind of Order" is a brilliant discussion of its subject.

To begin with, Kunitz traces the familiar ancestral lines of our present disorder—the destructive fragmentation of our world by Darwin, Marx, Freud, and Einstein in one arena; by Cezanne and Picasso, Rimbaud and Eliot, Whitman and Lawrence, Dostoevsky and Joyce in others (3). Hence, in our age "poetry inevitably tends to become increasingly aware of itself, to turn inward" (8), Kunitz writes, and like Heisenberg's demonstration "that the very act of observation changes the phenomena to be observed" (6), so "the work modifies the author . . . as a woman modifies herself in front of a mirror" (9). He thinks, Kunitz continues,

> . . . of those women in the paintings of de Kooning who sit in front of a window that is also a mirror and also a picture on a wall. How can you tell the inside from the outside, the reality from its reflection? Yeats had asked the question before, "How can we know the dancer from the dance?" (9)

However, "Since the art of our time is the only art we can get," it must be defended, and it can be, too, if one makes "the effort toward compassionate understanding . . ." (10). And, finally, in all its disorder, the art of our time wrestles through to "a kind of order," an order of the "greatest," one "which holds in suspension the most disorder; holds it in such precarious balance that each instant threatens its overthrow" (13). The material in this essay is heady and theoretical, abstract and knowledgeable. Its apothegms, of which I have quoted a few, and supporting examples and quotations make it an understandable and central statement of Kunitz's aesthetic ideas and also gloss his earlier lines in the poem "The Class Will Come to Order":

---

* "Our period demands a type of man who can restore the lost equilibrium between inner and outer reality . . . who can control his own existence by the process of balancing forces often regarded as irreconcilable: man in equipoise" ([3]; Kunitz's ellipsis).

Perhaps there's too much order in this world;
The poets love to haul disorder in,
Braiding their wrists with her long mistress hair,
And when the house is tossed about our ears,
The governors must set it right again.
How wise was he who banned them from his state!

(SP, 111)

The second essay in this part of the book, "The Search for a Style,"
is as short and to the point as the first was long and discursive. In
eight, mostly long, paragraphs Kunitz tries to clarify the style of an
age "so that its outlines become unmistakable" (14). The recent effort
to reject "academic verse and . . . to convert poetry into a popular
art . . . is doomed to fail" (15, 16), Kunitz asserts, because, in seeming
paradox, while a closed society such as that in Soviet Russia favors an
open, public poetry, an open society conversely tends to promote a
closed, private poetry: "where the poet is free to pursue his deepest
and most arcane thoughts and feelings to their source, his art tends to
embrace the personal and to prefer an intimate tone" (15).

Still, Kunitz adds, the contemporary work that "interests" him
"most . . . are poems that, stemming out of the great closed art of this
century, are nevertheless relaxed in the line, fluid in their development, organic in their form, and immediate in feeling. I begin to see
the possibility of a poetry that will recapture from the novel much of
the territory that has been forfeited to it" (16). So possibly poetry *has*
"become over-specialized, too different from prose" (16), and, as
Kunitz also said about his effort in teaching, "Why should not all men
of imagination feel that poetry is their medium, as long as they have a
language of the imagination to offer . . . ?" (16).

Following these two general essays on the conditions of poetry are
three others on specific subjects along with another general, theoretical essay. "A Visit to Russia" is mostly a narrative, with some
analysis, of his visit to the Soviet Union in 1967, making points about
the oppressiveness of the Soviet system under which, nonetheless,
poets and poetry flourish. As the Osip Mandelstam opening epigraph
to section 1 puts it, "Poetry is respected only in this country
[Russia]—people are killed for it" ([xiii]).

"On Translating Akhmatova" and "The Modernity of Keats"
derive from prefatory remarks to two of Kunitz's previous books, his
translations of Akhmatova and his selection from the poems and
letters of Keats. In the Keats essay Kunitz attempts to examine the

poetry without the encrustations of the years. "We do not clearly focus on the poets of the past," he writes,

> for we regard them through the eyeball of an ancestral giant who has already thumbed their pages, underscored their most sentimental passages, memorized their worst lines; and this Cyclopean organ with its superfluity of moisture, can scarcely be termed an ideal instrument of perception. (60)

He had had to fight himself free from "the idolatry" of his youth, and so has "been impelled to return intermittently to the pages of Keats as to a battlefield in the history of one man's taste, over which have raged certain small but savage wars" (60).

"Poet and State," the fifth essay in this first section, previously unpublished, returns to and expands on some of the themes in "A Kind of Order." Longer and more wide-ranging than that first essay, it implicitly continues the Herbert Marcuse epigraph for section 1: "Today the fight for life, the fight for Eros, is the *political* fight." Exploring connections between poet and state, "between good government and right words," Kunitz quotes Confucius's statement that language "matters above everything" (49) and contrasts that with the Platonic banishment of the poet from the state. For Plato, "the right words for the poet might be the wrong words for the state," especially the words of "the sons of Dionysus, the god of wine and ecstasy, as opposed to the rulers of the state, who are sons of Apollo, a relatively moderate divinity" (49–50).

"Among writers," Kunitz thinks, "the poet is freer than his brothers the novelist and playwright . . . more fortunate . . . than the contemporary painter or sculptor" because "nothing he can do will make his labor profitable" (52–53). He believes "that the shape of the future will be determined politically" (56). Thus some of "the causes that have agitated" Kunitz in what he calls "this unquiet century" in his "Foreword" ([xi]) covertly figure in this essay—anti-Semitism and Fascism. Overtly, the essay is about other matters: the indifference or even contempt with which poets are treated. "Even so fine a critical intellect as Edmund Wilson could ask," Kunitz writes, "'Does it really constitute a career for a man to do nothing but write lyric poetry?'" (56). In addition to the "impolite retort" which fortifies him but which he does not record, Kunitz wishes "that [former President] Nixon had been capable of reading Berryman's *Dream Songs*" (56).

The necessary full humanity for the poet would be an absolute awareness of the world and of the dangers around him with special attention to the dictum to "stay healthy in a sick world" (58). The charge Kunitz makes against the great writers who immediately preceded him—Joyce, Proust, Eliot, Frost, Stevens, Pound, and Yeats, too—is that they lacked wide sympathy: They cannot "be said to have cultivated their humanity, to have fulfilled themselves outside their art" (57). So "it was possible," Kunitz says, "a generation ago, . . . though I still find it hardly credible—to be both a reactionary and a poet, even a major poet" (55). Something like his own political position, that of a philosophical anarchist, he implies here, should be that of good and sane poets. Of the truly alive and "radiant" poets, Pasternak and William Carlos Williams, "it can be said that they did more than merely care about their art: they cared about others" (58). Yet, of course, "a poet isn't going to change the world with even the most powerful of his poems. The best he can reasonably hope for is to conquer a piece of himself" (58). But that, surely, he must constantly strive to do.

II   *Four for Roethke*

The four pieces on Theodore Roethke that make up section 2 of *A Kind of Order, A Kind of Folly* were published over a period of sixteen years and are a record of Kunitz's consistent high estimate of his friend's work. The first, the 1963 essay, "Remembering Roethke (1908–1963)," is an "in memoriam" piece. The second, "News of the Root," is a 1949 review of Roethke's *Lost Son*. The third, "The Taste of Self," from Ostroff's symposium *The Contemporary Poet as Artist and Critic*, is a 1961 close analysis of Roethke's "In a Dark Time." The fourth essay, "Poet of Transformations," is a magnificent coda, a consideration of Roethke's total achievement and especially a review of *The Far Field*, a posthumously published volume of Roethke's poems.

The first of these, a tender, autobiographical memoir, gauges the importance of Roethke to Kunitz himself—"The poet of my generation who meant most to me, in his person and in his art . . ." ([77])— and details their first meeting:

My recollection is of a traditionally battered jalopy from which a perfectly tremendous raccoon coat emerged, with my first book of poems tucked under its left paw. . . . The image that never left me was of a blond, smooth, shambling giant, irrevocably Teutonic, with a cold pudding of a face, somehow contradicted by the sullen downturn of the mouth and the pale furious eyes: a countenance ready to be touched by time, waiting to be transfigured, with a few subtle lines, into a tragic mask.   (78)

Kunitz and Roethke talked about poetry then and later; Kunitz suggested *Open House* as the title for Roethke's first book of poems (1941), a suggestion that Roethke both took and wrote a poem to go with the title as well (78). Kunitz, too, read Sir John Davies's *Orchestra* to Roethke and so began "Four for Sir John Davies," one of Roethke's important sequences (79). They played tennis together also and, later, croquet and badminton, and Kunitz introduced Roethke at his last reading in New York City at the Poetry Center in 1960 (79, 82).

In 1963 Kunitz continued to think of Roethke's *Lost Son* (1948) "as the great one" (80) of Roethke's books, and the 1949 review "News of the Root," the next essay, gives Kunitz's first reasons for so thinking: Roethke, he wrote then (1949), "stands among the original and powerful contemporary poets" ([83]). His "greenhouse world," Kunitz insisted, is not "rosy, innocent, optimistic. On the contrary, it swarms with malevolent forces" (84). And, he concluded, *The Lost Son*, "by virtue of its indomitable creativeness and audacity, includes much more chaos in its cosmos" than did *Open House*; "it is difficult, heroic, moving, and profoundly disquieting" (86).

In "The Taste of Self," a stanza-by-stanza analysis of Roethke's "In a Dark Time," Kunitz begins by making a connection with Gerard Manley Hopkins through Hopkins's "I taste *self* but at one tankard, that of my own being" (88). The self in Roethke, as Kunitz sees it, "is divided, and the hostile parts are seen as voraciously cannibalistic: 'My meat eats me'" (88). In the poem "In a Dark Time" itself, diction, line, and stanzaic units are tightly patterned, "fiercely won controls," which keep the poem from collapsing into "a cry, a tremendous outpouring of wordless agitation" (88).

In "his land of desolation," Kunitz writes, the speaker in the poem "struggles to recover his identity," seeks self-justification; in the motion-filled climax in stanza III, he dies to himself; and in IV, "returns to the prison-house of his senses" (89, 93). The strength and assurance of Kunitz's analysis here rest greatly on his thorough knowledge of Roethke's other poems, from which he quotes frequently, for "Roethke belongs," in Kunitz's estimation,

to that superior order of poets who will not let us rest in any one of their poems, who keep driving us back through the whole body of their work to that live cluster of images, ideas, memories, and obsessions that constitutes the individuating source of the creative personality, the nib of art, the very selfhood of the imagination.   (88)

The last of the "Four for Roethke" essays begins with a graceful retelling of the myth of Proteus and goes on to point out in Roethke's work transformations, shapeshiftings, transmutations, and metamorphoses. In Roethke's "most heroic enterprise, the sequence of interior monologues which he initiated with the title poem of *The Lost Son* . . . , continued in *Praise to the End* (1951), and which he persisted up to the last in returning to . . ." (100), he is "Proteus and all the forms of Proteus—flower, fish, reptile, amphibian, bird, dog, etc. . . ." (101). Ranging through Roethke's works and themes, Kunitz concludes with a detailed consideration of Roethke's *Far Field*, fifty new poems arranged by Roethke just before his death. Here Roethke "evokes his own valedictory image, Whitman is with him, and Prospero, and—in the shifting light Proteus, the old man of the sea, fatigued by his changes . . ." (108–109). Kunitz has high praise for these final words from Roethke.

III   *Root Images*

The third and most pleasing section of *A Kind of Order, A Kind of Folly* unites three mostly autobiographical pieces and concerns mainly Kunitz's interest in words and comments on two of his own poems. The first of these essays, "Swimming in Lake Chauggogagog-manchauggagogchabunagungamaugg," with a tongue-tangling title that is a compositor's nightmare, presents the time-honored picture of the precocious youngster's infatuation with words. For the Worcester-born Kunitz the magical word was the Indian name for nearby Lake Webster:

Chauggogagogmanchauggagogchabunagungamaugg. To think that this was reputed to be the longest lake-name in the world! To know, moreover, that this fantastic porridge of syllables made sense, and what delicious sense, signifying: "I-fish-on-my-side, you-fish-on-your-side, nobody-fishes-in-the-middle!" I practiced how to say it, priding myself on talking Indian . . . nor to this very day have I forgotten the combination.

([113]–14; Kunitz's ellipsis)

Giving this lake "its secret name," he says, "was somehow to possess it, to assert my power over the spot, as by an act of magic" (114).

Unfortunately, most of our words have lost their magical aspect, and the poet's problem is "how to make words potent and magical again, how to restore their lost vitality. . . . A poet is a man who yearns to swim in Lake Chauggogagogmanchauggagogchabunagungamaugg, not in Lake Webster" (114). For himself, Kunitz writes, he has "an ideal lyric" in his head "whose words flow together to form a single word-sentence, an unremitting stream of sound, as in the Indian lake-name; I am not reconciled to the knowledge that I shall never be able to write it" (114).

Meanwhile, how does a poet write his poems? Craft, will, solitude. Once asked what he considered to be his "chief asset as a poet," Kunitz answered, "'My ability to stay awake after midnight.' Perhaps," he goes on,

I was more serious than I intended. Certainly the poems of mine that I am most committed to are those that I recall fighting for hardest, through the anxious hours, until I managed to come out on the other side of fatigue, where I could begin to breathe again, as though the air had changed and I had found my second wind.   (115)

In illustration he tells, "not without trepidation," the story of the gestation of his 1953 poem "End of Summer," already retold above in Chapter 3.

"The Worcester Poets," the second of the essays in "Root Images," written as a Foreword to Michael True's brief study (forty-four pages), *Worcester Poets: With Notes toward a Literary History* (1972), gracefully comments on the curious fact that two of his "most admired colleagues"—Elizabeth Bishop and Charles Olson—"had at least a birthplace in common" with himself (118).

Suppose, I speculate, we had stayed home—what would have become of us? In that parochial climate, given our different backgrounds, would we have managed to find one another? All three of us, curiously, developed an inordinate love of place, but not of *that* place.   (118–19)

For Elizabeth Bishop it was Nova Scotia and, later, Brazil; for Olson, Gloucester; for Kunitz, the countryside, Connecticut, Bucks County, Pennsylvania, and Cape Cod. "Elizabeth and Charles were able to forget Worcester," Kunitz adds; "I doubt that I ever shall" (119).

Worcester for Kunitz is memories—Halley's Comet, school days, teachers, the public library, the art museum, the woods beyond his house. Tantalizingly, he notes that he has "much, much more to tell, but this is scarcely the proper occasion for spilling everything" (121). Some day, he promises, he "must set down, if only as a chapter of Americana, the narrative of my horse-and-buggy adventures, when I was lamplighter on the Quinapoxet roads" (121). He ends by quoting the one sentence that makes up the three stanzas of the concluding half of "Goose Pond," a 1956 poem in which the protagonist "meets his childhood beating back/ To find what furies made him man" (121).

The third essay in section 3 is the one on Kunitz's own poem "Father and Son" from the symposium on that poem in Anthony Ostroff's *Contemporary Poet as Artist and Critic*. This essay, short to the point of terseness, candidly admits to dream as the starting point for the poem and adds a few illuminating details. He wrote about the poem reluctantly, Kunitz confesses at the end of the essay, because he is "fearful of surrendering to the temptation of saying more than I should" (127). Anyway, "Once a poem has been distributed, it is no longer the property of the poet" (123) and "the words of the poem stand forever separate from the words about it . . ." (127). The poet "has already had his chance" (127).

IV   *Sections 4 through 7 of* A Kind of Order

Since the first three parts of *A Kind of Order, A Kind of Folly* are the most important in my judgment, I have surveyed them in some detail. Now I shall glance briefly at sections 4 through 7, before examining the concluding part 8, "Recapitulations." These thirty-five pieces in the middle of the book are good reading in themselves—I know no better single article on Robert Lowell than the "Conversation" in "Tête-à-Tête"—but the variety here is too great and some of the items themselves too brief (but four or five paragraphs) for any organized individual comment.

The first of these sections, 4, "Studio Life," has as its theme the close relationship between poets and artists. In "The Sister Arts" Kunitz makes the admission that he prefers "the company of painters and sculptors to that of poets" because poets "tend to be rather surly and withdrawn," while artists "are temperamentally gregarious" ([131]). And while they greatly enjoy each other's company, artists seem to like to have poets around too, as such poet-artist friendships as Keats-Haydon, Baudelaire-Delacroix, Rilke-Rodin, and others testify (132). Poet-painters and painter-poets, combining in one being both talents, are further "evidence of the natural affinity between poet and painter . . ." (132). The outstanding examples are Michelangelo and Blake and also the Chinese masters Wang Wei and Buson (132).

But, as Kunitz says, getting to the point of his essay, introducing a portfolio of contemporary poems chosen and illustrated by American painters, the "contemporary western artist . . . lacks a . . . convention" (133) comparable to that in the Orient of *haiku* and *haiga*, poem and picture inextricably entwined, and what is he to do with a self-sufficient poem? An artist does not illustrate it merely, but "must invent a style of graphic translation that enables him to register his variable sense of the poem" (133). Today, Kunitz concludes, "while the style of an age, or at least of a generation, is evolving, it seems to me imperative that poets and painters should continue their civilized discourse" (134).

Besides his reflections on having his head sculpted by James Rosati, the section on "Studio Life" also contains a long essay on "The Temptations of the Artist" and a short, moving tribute to Kunitz's friend the artist Mark Rothko. The one is an informed survey of recent trends in art, with remarks on the overexpanded role of the critic and an inveighing against the "dehumanization of art." Rothko, the artist who took his own life in 1970, was, in Kunitz's view, "a poet among painters"; to describe Rothko's work Kunitz quotes from his own extensively revised poem from 1930, "Among the Gods": "Shapes of things interior to Time,/Hewn out of chaos when the Pure was plain" (149; SP, 7).

Following the two "Conversations," one with Robert Lowell and the other with Andrei Voznesensky, of part 5 of *A Kind of Order*, is "Works and Lives," part 6, an anthology of reviews of various works of some twenty or so poets ranging, alphabetically, from Conrad Aiken to William Carlos Williams. Mostly quite short these are confined in subject matter to the particular works reviewed. Part 7 collects five of Kunitz's introductions to the works of the "Younger Poets" that he selected for inclusion in the Yale Series; these are models of essays of this kind, biographical, judiciously analytical, kindly, and accurate. Each isolates each poet's strengths, places him in a tradition, makes judgments about the worth of his accomplishment, and, if faulty, is so in an overgenerosity of praise. Indeed, in a certain sense, though these five essays are quite good in themselves, placed together as they are here, they make this the least interesting part of *A Kind of Order*. For Hugh Seidman, Peter Klappert,

Michael Casey, Robert Hass, and Michael Ryan are at the moment little-known poets, a condition time may correct, but now without the support of the poems that follow in the books in the series, these introductions are too brief to be thoroughly convincing.

V *Recapitulations*

The eighth and final section of Kunitz's prose book is made up of one item entitled "Seedcorn and Windfall," a collection of observations, thoughts, and ruminations taken from "notebooks, articles, and transcripts of interviews" ([297]). The nouns of the title point to the use for and the characteristics of what is here: "Seedcorn" is corn set aside for planting a new crop; so some of these paragraphs might later grow into something else. "Windfall" is something blown down by the wind, as fruit from a tree; so some of these comments are accidental accumulations of a lifetime.

Engrossing reading, "Seedcorn and Windfall" does not lend itself to analysis or summary; what I can say is that almost all of it is good. An occasional aphorism may seem glib or even mechanical: "An old poet ought never to be caught with his technique showing" (307). "I have no religion—perhaps that is why I think so much about God" (308). Mainly, though, notations are stringent and memorable: "I have no patience with the Midas-fingered who complain that poetry resists being turned into gold. It is better than gold" (300). "You don't know why you're writing poems, any more than a cat knows why it claws at the bark of a tree" (300). "To remain a poet after forty requires an awareness of your darkest Africa, that part of your self that will never be tamed" (301). "If we did not wear masks, we should be frightened of mirrors" (305). "People don't have to be taught to suffer—they have to be taught how to live" (305).

A "seedcorn" might be such a passage as this one:

In the beginning Nature threatened Man. Now their roles are reversed. Is there anything on earth more to be feared than the hairless biped *homo sapiens*, the beast that knows so much and loves so little?   (303–304)

Another seedcorn might be the anecdote about the foundered whale on Cape Cod who

. . . was lying there, in monstrous desolation, making the most terrifying noises—rumbling—groaning. I put my hands on his flanks and I could feel the life inside him. And while I was standing there, suddenly he opened his eye. It was a big, red, cold eye, and it was staring directly at me. A shudder of recognition passed between us. Then the eye closed forever.   (306)

The simplicity and exactness of the language here, this planed, plain prose without tropes, characterizes the writing of many parts of this final piece of *A Kind of Order, A Kind of Folly.*

"Seedcorn and Windfall" is, then, finally, a splendid piece with which to end the book. No organized essay could offer as much—sixteen pages of reflective wisdom, autobiographical information, and a muted melancholy of tone aptly caught in the epigraph from Sappho: "The moon has set, and the Pleiades; it is the middle of the night and time passes, time passes, and I lie alone" ([297]). Seventy, the aging poet is mellower but not mellowed, not serene, still unreconciled to "the good-enough that spoils the world" (SP, 75). He is, he says, "moving toward a more expansive universe," and he proposes "to take more risks" than he ever did before (312). "Seedcorn and Windfall" is a risk, a fine risk well worth taking.

CHAPTER 8

Conclusion

W HEN Stanley Kunitz was appointed Consultant in Poetry to the Library of Congress for 1974–1975 and reappointed in 1975–1976, he went on leave from his teaching at Columbia University and commuted between New York and Washington to arrange readings and recordings, and to attend to the other duties of his post, introducing writers, organizing conferences, and giving talks. He made an extensive lecture and reading tour to the West Coast of Africa in 1976 and returned to his teaching duties at Columbia after his Consultantship ended. He also resigned as editor of the Yale Younger Poets in 1977 and worked as editor and co-translator of *Orchard Lamps* by the Ukrainian poet Ivan Drach (1978). He taught creative writing at Princeton as Senior Fellow in the Humanities for a term in 1978 and subsequently returned once more to Columbia University.

Not yet can Kunitz have a final word said about him or his work. Still to end this study, I can make some concluding remarks. Clearly my own assessment of what he did is high. Some of his recent work that I have seen seems different from any that he has previously done.[1] A mid-1970s poem, "Words for the Unknown Makers," inspired by a show of American folk art at the Whitney Museum of American Art in 1974, is quite strikingly unlike any of his previous work. In five parts, four of them verse, and one prose, it has, especially in the prose poem, "A Blessing of Women," a voice new to Kunitz. The seven parts of this prose piece name five American women of the last century who worked at what materials they had at hand to adorn the world. Kunitz remembers and "blesses" them and their sisters with great tenderness, as in these last two sections:

BLESS IN A CONGREGATION,
because they are so numerous, those industrious schoolgirls stitching their alphabets; and the deft ones with needles at lacework, crewel, knitting; and mistresses of spinning, weaving, dyeing; and daughters of tinsmiths painting

their ornamental mottoes; and hoarders of rags hooking and braiding their rugs; and adepts in cutouts, valentines, stencils, still lifes, and "fancy pieces"; and middle-aged housewives painting, for the joy of it, landscapes and portraits; and makers of bedcovers with names that sing in the night—Rose of Sharon, Princess Feather, Delectable Mountains, Turkey Tracks, Drunkard's Path, Indiana Puzzle, Broken Dishes, Star of LeMoyne, Currants and Coxcomb, Rocky-Road-to-Kansas.

> BLESS THEM AND GREET THEM
> as they pass from their long obscurity, through the gate that separates us from our history, a moving rainbow-cloud of witnesses in a rising hubbub, jubilantly turning to greet one another, this tumult of sisters.[2]

Succeeding as it does the personal pain and perfection of the unflinchingly mature poems of *The Testing-Tree*, a gentle, evocative, impersonal poem like "Words for the Unknown Makers" signified something quite new in Kunitz's work.

A collected volume of Kunitz's complete poems in the planning for four or five years was published in July 1979 too late for consideration in my text. Entitled *The Poems of Stanley Kunitz, 1928-1978*, it has a section of poems written since *The Testing-Tree* under the title "The Layers," after a poem published in the January-February issue of *American Poetry Review* in 1979.[3] This 44-lined poem in a single section of short lines, seems a recollection over a long life and a valedictory. The persona, an "I" once again, is "directed" by "a nimbus-clouded voice" to

> "Live in the layers,
> not on the litter."

Both "layers" and "litter" seem to be Kunitz's rather usual wordplay with double meanings. The poem ends,

> Though I lack the art
> to decipher it,
> no doubt the next chapter
> in my book of transformations
> is already written.
> I am not done with my changes.

Four recent poems in the *Atlantic* (January 1979), "The Unquiet Ones," "My Sisters," "The Quarrel," and "The Catch" are like this poem, "The Layers," and like some of the best short poems in *The*

Testing-Tree, unsparingly honest, precise in image, short in line, with simple language brought to an exalted height in meaning. "The Catch," the title again with a double meaning, ends,

> You may look, child,
> all you want.
> This prize belongs to no one.
> But you will pay all
> your life for the privilege,
> all your life.[4]

As it is now, without the newer poems that this book of collected poems contains, Kunitz's work consists already of a few nearly perfect poems of great intensity, passion, and universality and a further body of good poems that ensure his reputation. Besides all these, his book of essays and conversations, rather neglected so far, and his translations from Russian round out a long, busy life that was remarkable in its single-minded dedication to poetry. Underlying everything he has done is his conviction as to the seriousness of poetry: "Like Hopkins' bird of peace, a poem does not come to coo; it comes with work to do." Kunitz's own life has been, in his phrase about Keats's, not a career but "a life of poetry."

Notes and References

Preface

1. The Auden and Kunitz quotations are in David Lupher, "Stanley Kunitz on Poetry: A Yale Lit Interview," *Yale Literary Magazine*, 136 (May 1968), 13. Hereafter referred to as *Yale Literary Magazine*.
2. John Wakeman, ed., *World Authors, 1950-1970* (New York, 1975), p. 825. Hereafter, *World Authors*.
3. Both the critic's observation and Kunitz's "fortunately not true!" comment are in the Kunitz entry in *Contemporary Authors*, vols. 41-44.
4. "American Poetry's Silver Age," *Harper's*, 219 (October 1959), 174. In 1959 the poets who had "remained relatively obscure" or "undervalued" were Phelps Putnam, John Peale Bishop, H. D., Laura Riding, Edward Dahlberg, Charles Olson, Kenneth Rexroth, Robert Penn Warren, Yvor Winters, Theodore Roethke, Jean Garrigue, J. V. Cunningham, John Berryman, and Howard Nemerov.
5. "Process and Thing: A Year of Poetry," *Harper's*, 221 (September 1960), 104.
6. "The New Books," *Harper's*, 223 (August 1961), 87.
7. *Selected Poems* (Boston, 1958), p. 13. Hereafter, SP; citation in text and footnote to Kunitz's other books of poetry will be by initials also: IT—*Intellectual Things* (New York, 1930); PW—*Passport to the War* (New York, 1944); TT—*The Testing-Tree* (Boston, 1971).

Chapter One

1. *World Authors*, p. 822. Unless otherwise documented the factual details in this chapter have been compiled from the Kunitz entry in this work, that in *Current Biography*, 1959, and from information supplied by Kunitz himself.
2. *World Authors*, p. 823.
3. *Wilson Library Bulletin*, 16 (November 1941), 261; 17 (February 1943), 464; and 29 (November 1954), 251.
4. Quoted in *World Authors*, p. 824.
5. Ibid.
6. "Craft Interview with Stanley Kunitz," *New York Quarterly*, 1 (Fall 1970), 19. Hereafter, *New York Quarterly*.
7. Ibid., p. 17.

8. *World Authors*, pp. 822–823.

9. Public discussion, Burlington, Vermont, November 13, 1973.

10. The quotations are from a public discussion (as immediately above). See also Michael Ryan, "An Interview with Stanley Kunitz," *Iowa Review*, 5 (Spring 1974), 81. Hereafter, *Iowa Review*.

The poems in the *Dial* are "Death in Moonlight" and "Geometry of Moods," 86 (February 1929), 116–17. Both of these poems were included in IT, 31 and 2–3; "Geometry," SP, 21.

Some of the other poems published at this time are "Change," *Commonweal*, 9 (January 23, 1929), 350 (in IT and SP); "Very Tree," *Commonweal*, 10 (September 11, 1929), 40 (in IT, not in SP); "Enormous Night," *Commonweal*, 11 (November 27, 1929), 107 (not reprinted); "Soul's Adventure," *New Republic*, 61 (December 18, 1929), 98 (in IT; in SP as "The Pivot"); in *Poetry*, nine poems: "A Daughter of the Sun Is She," "First Love," "Last Words," "The Moon at the Door," "Poem," "Postscript," "Prophecy on Lethe," "Twilight," and "Vita Nuova," *Poetry*, 34 (July 1929), 181–89 (only the third of these has not been reprinted; the others are in IT and all but the first two are in SP); "Interior," *Nation*, 130 (April 16, 1930), 452 (not reprinted); "Invocation to the Phoenix," *Nation*, 130 (May 21, 1930), 601 (as "Invocation" in PW and SP): "Man Does Not Ask for Much," *Nation*, 127 (August 22, 1928), 182 (not reprinted); "Parting," *Nation*, 130 (January 22, 1930), 100 (in IT, not in SP); "Skull of Ecstasy," *Nation*, 130 (June 25, 1930), 735 (not reprinted; some lines salvaged for "Among the Gods" in SP).

11. (Boston, 1975), p. 301. Hereafter referred to as *A Kind of Order*.

12. "Process and Thing," *Harper's*, 221 (September 1960), 102.

13. *New York Quarterly*, p. 13.

14. *Iowa Review*, p. 85.

15. *New York Quarterly*, p. 13.

16. *Iowa Review*, p. 80.

17. *Wilson Library Bulletin*, 17 (May 1943), 756.

18. "An Interview with Stanley Kunitz—*Conducted by Cynthia Davis*," *Contemporary Literature*, 15 (Winter 1974), 5. Henceforth referred to as *Contemporary Literature*.

19. *Poems of Akhmatova* (Boston, 1973), p. 129.

20. *Iowa Review*, pp. 80–81.

21. Ibid., p. 80.

22. The quotations and the facts about contracts and tenure are from *World Authors*, pp. 823–24 and from *Iowa Review*, pp. 80–81.

23. *Iowa Review*, p. 81.

24. *A Kind of Order*, p. 303.

25. *Iowa Review*, p. 85.

26. "The Seminar in the Arts," *Education*, 73 (November 1952), 17.

27. "Andrei Voznesensky and Stanley Kunitz: A Conversation," *Antaeus*, 6 (Summer 1972), 126.

28. *Iowa Review*, p. 78.

29. *Commonweal,* 69 (February 12, 1959), 524.
30. *Iowa Review,* p. 80.
31. *Wilson Library Bulletin,* 34 (September 1959), 73.
32. *Contemporary Literature,* p. 11.
33. *Iowa Review,* p. 83.
34. Ibid.
35. Ibid., p. 80.
36. *A Kind of Order,* p. 307.
37. Most of the quotations and information in this section on influences are from the interviews in *Iowa Review,* pp. 76–77; *Contemporary Literature,* p. 13; *New York Quarterly,* pp. 17–18; and from *World Authors, 1950–1970,* p. 822.

Chapter Two

1. *Poetry,* 60 (July 1942), 215.
2. *Contemporary Literature,* p. 13.
3. The quotations are from ibid., pp. 13–14.
4. *Yale Literary Magazine,* p. 9.
5. Ibid.
6. *Contemporary Literature,* p. 6.
7. Jean H. Hagstrum, "The Poetry of Stanley Kunitz: An Introductory Essay" in *Poets in Progress,* ed. Edward Hungerford (Evanston, Ill., 1967), p. 45.
8. Ibid.
9. Ibid., p. 46.
10. For the text of a poem from either *Intellectual Things* or *Passport to the War,* whenever possible I cite *Selected Poems* because that book is in print as the other two are not; usually a poem is little revised from its appearance in the earlier book.
11. *Contemporary Literature,* p. 10.
12. Hagstrum, p. 46.
13. Ibid., p. 43.
14. *World Authors,* p. 822.
15. Ibid.
16. The poems are "Vita Nuova," "My Surgeons," "Night Letter," "The Illusionist," and "The Fitting of the Mask," SP, 109, 73, 102, 78, and 82. The final quotation is from "What of the Night?" a poem which I read in a typescript supplied me by Kunitz.
17. Plato, *Republic,* Book X, concluding passage.
18. The "Florentine" he invented, Kunitz has said; the word originally was "epicene," referring to Marcel Proust. Not caring for the sound of "epicene," he changed it to "Florentine." The anecdote refers to Proust's attempt to revise the death scene of Bergotte in *La Prisonniere.* Painter's biography quotes Proust as saying, "Now I'm in the same condition, I want to add some

notes to the death of Bergotte." George D. Painter, *Proust: The Later Years* (Boston, 1965), p. 360.

19. Hagstrum, p. 43.

20. Ibid., p. 47. The details are, respectively, from "Change," "Geometry of Moods," "Twilight," "Ambergris," "Lovers Relentlessly," and "The Words of the Preacher," in SP, 65, 21, 50, 74, 20, and 51.

21. From "Prophecy on Lethe," "Organic Bloom," and "Beyond Reason," in SP, 61, 57, and 9.

22. From SP, 80, 84, and 73.

23. From SP, 47, 75, and 112.

24. *Nation*, 187 (October 11, 1958), 214.

25. *Contemporary Literature*, p. 11.

26. Ibid., p. 7.

27. *Nation*, 213 (September 20, 1971), 251. Other less successful "religious" poems are "Soul's Adventure," "Enormous Night," "Deciduous Branch," and "The Words of the Preacher." "Soul's Adventure" is in SP as "The Pivot," p. 62. "Enormous Night" was not reprinted from its appearance in *Commonweal*, 11 (November 27, 1929), 107. The other two are in SP, 52 and 51.

28. *Poetry*, 60 (July 1942), 215.

29. "Kunitz, Stanley (Jasspon)," in *Contemporary Poets of the English Language*, ed. Rosalie Murphy (New York, 1970), p. 620.

30. *Poetry*, 34 (July 1929), 189

31. *Poetry*, 58 (June 1941), 153.

32. *Contemporary Literature*, p. 12.

Chapter Three

1. Wallace Stevens, "The Man with the Blue Guitar," *The Collected Poems of Wallace Stevens* (New York, 1975), p. 176. The 1972 interview, published in 1974, is that in *Contemporary Literature*, p. 8.

2. The quotations about Kunitz's method of writing poems are gathered from *Iowa Review*, pp. 78 and 85, and "Andrei Voznesensky and Stanley Kunitz: A Conversation," *Antaeus*, 6 (Summer 1972), 126. Hereafter cited as "Voznesensky and Kunitz."

3. The subsequent quotations about the writing of "End of Summer" are from *A Kind of Order*, pp. 115–17.

4. "Auden on Poetry: A Conversation," *Atlantic*, 218 (August 1966), 94.

5. *Yale Literary Magazine*, p. 6.

6. The foregoing quotations are from Robert Russell, "The Poet in the Classroom," *College English*, 28 (May 1967), 582.

7. *A Kind of Order*, p. 300.

8. *Nation*, 130 (May 21, 1930), 601.

9. *Nation*, 130 (June 25, 1930), 735.

10. "Los" is Blake's name for the Holy Spirit, the third person of the Trinity. Blake's poem, untitled, is in a letter to Thomas Butts, 22 November

1802. *The Poetry and Prose of William Blake*, ed. David V. Erdman with commentary by Harold Bloom (Garden City, New York, 1970), pp. 692–93.
11. Kunitz's words, quoted in Hagstrum, p. 55.
12. Ibid., pp. 52–53.
13. The four "Blakean" poems are "The Waltzer in the House," "The Way Down," "As Flowers Are," and "When the Light Falls," SP, 13, 106, 10, 6. Hagstrum, p. 53.
14. The lines quoted are in SP, 112, 41, 31, 83, and 26.
15. The lines quoted are in SP, 48, 55, and 16.
16. The lines quoted are in SP, 46, 116, and 46.
17. Northrop Frye, *Anatomy of Criticism: Four Essays* (New York, 1969), p. 280.
18. Ibid., p. 281.
19. The lines quoted are in SP, 94, 46, 21, and 48.
20. See Roland John, "[A review of *The Terrible Threshold*]," *Agenda*, 13 (Summer 1975), 62, and the essays on "Father and Son" in Anthony Ostroff, *The Contemporary Poet as Artist and Critic* (Boston 1964), Robert Beloof, p. 69 and Robert Lowell, p. 73.
21. Robert Lowell, "On Stanley Kunitz's 'Father and Son,'" in Ostroff, p. 73.
22. Stanley Kunitz, "On Stanley Kunitz's 'Father and Son,'" Ostroff, p. 78.
23. Ibid.
24. *Encylopaedia Judaica*, Vol. 10, p. 1293.
25. *New York Quarterly*, p. 17.
26. *A Kind of Order*, p. 114.
27. The lines quoted are in SP, 54, 56, 73, 75, and 76.
28. SP, 102, 23, 23, 24, 53, and 68.
29. "Minatory" is in TT, 63. The other words are in SP, 16, 26, 61, 106, and 36.
30. Hugh Kenner, *A Homemade World: The American Modernist Writers* (New York, 1975), p. xi.
31. SP, 26 and 31.
32. The quotations and information about Kunitz's gardening and his living in the countryside, not the city, are gathered from Kunitz himself; *Current Biography*, p. 243; *Yale Literary Magazine*, p. 12; "Auden on Poetry," p. 100; Robin Brantley, "A Touch of the Poet," *New York Times Magazine*, September 7, 1975, pp. 80–83.
33. SP, 89–90. Robert Lowell, "To the Reader," in *Imitations* (New York, 1961), pp. 46–47.

Chapter Four

1. *Contemporary Literature*, p. 11.
2. *Iowa Review*, p. 76; *Contemporary Literature*, p. 4.

3. *Contemporary Literature*, p. 3.

4. Ibid., pp. 2–3.

5. Pliny the Younger, Epistles I.9.1. See also Pythagoras, *Aurea Carmina* 42.

6. *Contemporary Literature*, p. 4.

7. M. L. Rosenthal, *The New Poets: American and British Poetry Since World War II* (New York, 1967), pp. 6 and 10.

8. *Contemporary Literature*, p. 14.

9. Rosenthal, *New Poets*, p. 15.

10. The phrase "The Serpent's Word" comes from the poem "The Dark and the Fair," SP, 34; "The Terrible Threshold," from "Open the Gates," SP, 41; "Prince of Counterfeits," from "The Fitting of the Mask," SP, 83; "A World to Lose," from "The Last Picnic," SP, 93; and "The Coat Without a Seam," from "The Way Down," SP, 106.

11. Paul Engle and Joseph Langland, eds., *Poet's Choice* (New York, 1962), p. 68.

12. Ibid., p. xiii.

13. *Contemporary Literature*, p. 5.

14. Ibid.

15. *Contemporary American Poetry* (New York, 1966), pp. 44–47.

16. Ibid., p. 46.

17. An "open city" is one which is "a military objective but is completely demilitarized and left open to enemy occupation in order to gain immunity, under international law, from bombardment and attack."

18. *Iowa Review*, p. 77.

19. In John, 19:23–24. The outer coat worn by the High Priest is woven as one piece without a seam. In the Rabbinic tradition God gave Adam an unstitched coat and after him Moses and the High Priest. When the tradition was taken over into Christian theology the Adam-Moses-Redeemer typology applied it also to Christ.

20. Russell, "Poet in the Classroom," p. 584.

21. Ibid.

22. The one-paragraph prose section (IV) of *Vita Nuova*, of which this is the last sentence, concerns Dante's wasting away with love and being questioned about it by his friends: "And I, perceiving their evil questioning, through the will of Love, who commanded me according to the counsel of the reason, replied to them, that it was Love who had brought me to this pass. I spoke of Love, because I bore on my face so many of his signs that this could not be concealed. And when they asked me: 'For whom has Love thus wasted thee?' I, smiling, looked at them and said nothing." Charles Eliot Norton, trans., *The New Life of Dante Alighieri* (Boston, 1898), p. 7.

Part of one line in the last section of the poem, "The lesson for today," is identical to the title of Robert Frost's earlier 1941 Harvard Phi Beta Kappa poem. I do not perceive any important connections between the two poems such as to suggest that Kunitz might have been alluding in any way to the

Frost poem. The two poems have some similarities of subject, poetry, the state, and the world; Frost's poem is much longer (161 lines), is rhymed, and "rides no beast of action." Frost's "lesson for today/Is how to be unhappy yet polite." The poem ends with Frost's memorable epitaph, "I had a lover's quarrel with the world." The phrase, "The lesson for today," is sufficiently everyday for the identity to be coincidental. "The Lesson for Today," *The Complete Poems of Robert Frost* (New York, 1964), pp. 471–476.

23. Harvey Gross, *Sound and Form in Modern Poetry: A Study of Prosody from Thomas Hardy to Robert Lowell* (Ann Arbor, Mich., 1968), p. 280.

24. *A Kind of Order*, p. 50.

25. Gross, pp. 279 and 280. Gross's reading is "Brai ding| their wrists| with her long mis | tress hair. . . ."

26. Ibid., p. 326.

27. "American Poetry's Silver Age," *Harper's*, 219 (June 1959), 178.

28. *Yale Literary Magazine*, p. 9.

Chapter Five

1. *Contemporary Literature*, p. 12.

2. Ibid., p. 11.

3. Stanley Moss, "[A review of *The Testing-Tree*]," *Nation*, 213 (September 20, 1971), 251.

4. Michael True, *Worcester Poets. With Notes Toward a Literary History* (Worcester, Mass., 1972), p. 28.

5. *A Kind of Order*, p. 119.

6. Ibid., p. 305. Kunitz's ellipsis.

7. David Huddle, "In Fierce Decay a Stripe of Honey: The Poetry of Stanley Kunitz," *Northern New England Review*, 1 (1975), 21.

8. Moss, p. 250.

9. The allusion is to Coleridge's "The Nightingale. A Conversation Poem, April, 1798," a blank verse poem of 110 anecdotal lines. The reference is to lines 98–105:

> . . . and once, when he awoke
> In most distressful mood (some inward pain
> Had made up that strange thing, an infant's dream—)
> I hurried with him to our orchard-lot,
> And he beheld the moon, and, hushed at once,
> Suspends his sobs, and laughs most silently,
> While his fair eyes, that swam with undropped tears,
> Did glitter in the yellow moon-beam!

The lines are remembered inexactly, for it is not Coleridge who is "heavy-hearted," but the child. Also the verb "Suspends" has been transferred from "sobs" to "tear" and "glitter" has been transformed into "a sparkling moon," a sea-change that is for the better.

10. TT, 8–9. The periods of ellipsis are in the poem.

11. Huddle, p. 25.

12. Moss, p. 231.

13. *Iowa Review*, pp. 78, 77.

14. *World Authors*, p. 822.

15. See, among other songbooks, *Songs We Love to Sing, Songs for Every Purpose and Occasion for Home, School and Assembly Use* (Chicago, 1938).

16. *A Kind of Order*, pp. 311–12.

17. Moss, p. 250.

18. Dietrich Bonhoeffer, *The Cost of Discipleship*, trans. Reginald H. Fuller with a memoir by G. Leibholz (New York, 1963), p. 47.

19. Dietrich Bonhoeffer, *Letters and Papers from Prison*, ed. Eberhard Bethge, trans. Reginald H. Fuller (New York, 1967), p. 41.

20. Eberhard Bethge, *Dietrich Bonhoeffer: Man of Vision, Man of Courage*, trans. Eric Mosbacher, Peter and Betty Ross, Frank Clarke, and William Glen-Doepel (New York, 1970), p. 685. The camp doctor's letter is quoted on p. 830.

21. Moss, p. 231.

22. Brantley, p. 80.

23. For "the King of the Wood" see the first chapter of Sir James George Frazer, *The Golden Bough: A Study in Magic and Religion* (London, 1911–15).

24. The poem from SP is "The Economist's Song," *The Terrible Threshold*, p. 12, SP, 100.

25. Also omitted from *The Terrible Threshold* are "This Day This World," "Invocation," and "No Word," PW, 21, 23, and 24.

26. The omitted translations are "Bolsheviks—*from Aba Stolzenberg*" and the three Akhmatova poems, TT, 44, 51, 53, and 54.

27. *Contemporary Literature*, p. 9.

28. Ibid.

29. Ibid., p. 8.

30. Ibid., p. 7.

31. Ibid.

Chapter Six

1. "The New Books," *Harper's*, 223 (August 1961), 90.

2. "A Note on the Translations," *Poems of Akhmatova* (Boston, 1973), p. 29.

3. *Contemporary Literature*, p. 11.

4. TT, 51. In *Poems of Akhmatova*, the semicolon at the end of the first quoted line has been changed to a colon, p. 83. The echo of Dickens seems to be a "liberty" Kunitz takes in this stanza; Akhmatova's line ends with a question mark. Richard McKane translates it, "Who has got lost two steps

from home,/where the snow is waist deep and an end to all?" *Anna Akhmatova: Selected Poems*, trans. with an Introduction by Richard McKane (London, 1969), p. 72.

5. Sam N. Driver, *Anna Akhmatova* (New York, 1972), p. 28.

6. Andrei Voznesensky, *Story Under Full Sail*, trans. Stanley Kunitz with Vera Reck, Maureen Sager, Catherine Leach (Garden City, New York, 1974).

7. "A Note on the Translations," *Poems of Akhmatova*, p. 31.

8. Ibid., pp. 29–30.

9. "Translating Akhmatova," *New York Review of Books*, August 9, 1973, pp. 9–10.

10. The quotations are from pp. 51, 57, 71, 73, 75, and 87. The compared translations are Eugene M. Kayden's, *Colorado Quarterly*, 20 (Winter 1972), 406, and Richard McKane's, p. 38.

11. *Poems of Akhmatova*, p. 19.

12. "From a Letter to N.," trans. Carl R. Proffer, *Russian Literature Triquarterly*, Number 1 (Fall 1971), 48–49.

13. *Poems of Akhmatova*, p. 151. This passage is one of the three italicized sections in the excerpt.

14. Carl R. Proffer, "*A Poem without a Hero:* Notes and Commentary," *Russian Literature Triquarterly*, Number 1 (Fall 1971), 47.

15. Driver, p. 125.

16. Ibid.; Carl R. Proffer, trans., "A Poem without a Hero," *Russian Literature Triquarterly*, Number 1 (Fall 1971), 28; The "embers" passage is quoted in "The Unshackled Voice," A. Sinyavsky's essay in Richard McKane's *Anna Akhmatova: Selected Poems*, p. 15.

17. Brodsky, p. 10.

18. "[A review of *Poems of Akhmatova*]," *Poetry*, 124 (July 1974), 238.

19. Some important translations of Akhmatova are these: D. M. Thomas, trans., *Anna Akhmatova: Requiem and Poem Without a Hero* (Athens, Ohio, 1977); Vladimir Markov and Merrill Sparks, eds., *Modern Russian Poetry* (New York, 1967), 26 of Akhmatova's poems; Richard McKane's translation already cited, 58 poems; Eugene M. Kayden, trans., "Seven Poems: Anna Akhmatova (1889–1966)," *Colorado Quarterly*, 20 (Spring 1972), 530–34; Eugene M. Kayden, trans., "Sixteen Poems: Anna Akhmatova (1889–1966)," *Colorado Quarterly*, 22 (Autumn 1973), 278–88; Carl R. Proffer with Assya Humesky, trans., "A Poem without a Hero," *Russian Literature Triquarterly*, Number 1 (Fall 1971), 21–46. This last item has also been published as a book (New York: Ardis, 1973). Other translations of "Poems of Anna Akhmatova" by Jamie Fuller, Carl R. Proffer, and Barbara Heidt Monter appear in the *Russian Literature Triquarterly*, Number 1 (Fall 1971), 15–20. The Robert Lowell and Olga Carlisle translations appear in *Poets on Street Corners* (New York, 1968), pp. 60–73.

20. Quoted in *Times Literary Supplement*, July 10, 1969, p. 751, and in *Choice*, 10 (October 1973), 1202.

21. "Process and Thing: A Year of Poetry," *Harper's*, 221 (September 1960), 101.

22. Born Anna Andreevna Gorenko, Akhmatova chose her grandmother's name, Akhmatova, Tartar in origin, as her pseudonym.

23. *Poems of Akhmatova*, p. 31. "Tragedy did not wither her" of course links Akhmatova with Shakespeare's Cleopatra, the subject of one of Akhmatova's poems.

24. "Notes on the Poems," *Poems of Akhmatova*, p. 165.

25. *Library Journal*, 98 (June 15, 1973), 1923.

26. Brodsky, p. 10.

27. "A Poem without a Hero," *Russian Literature Triquarterly*, Number 1 (Fall 1971), p. 27.

28. "Notes and Commentary," ibid., p. 47.

29. Helen Muchnic, "Poems of Akhmatova," *New York Times Book Review*, October 21, 1973, p. 6.

30. Richard McKane, p. 91.

31. *Contemporary Literature*, p. 11.

32. Michael Mesic, p. 238.

33. Muchnic, p. 6.

34. Brodsky, p. 10.

35. Vladimir Markov, "Preface," *Modern Russian Poetry*, ed. and trans. by Vladimir Markov and Merrill Sparks (New York, 1967), p. lxxix.

Chapter Seven

1. *A Kind of Order, A Kind of Folly: Essays and Conversations* (Boston 1975), p. [xi]. Hereafter in this chapter, page references to this book are in parentheses following each citation.

2. Richard Vine, "The Language that Saves," *Salmagundi*, No. 36 (Winter 1977), 122-3.

3. Ibid., p. 118.

4. Ibid.

Chapter Eight

1. "Words for the Unknown Makers," *Craft Horizons*, 34 (February 1974), 32-39. The five unnumbered parts are entitled "Job," "Sacred to the Memory," "A Blessing of Women," "Girl with Sampler," and "Trompe l'Oeil." With the exception of "A Blessing of Women," each is accompanied by a photograph of a piece of folk art from the exhibition. Another new work is a collage/poem, "The Crystal Cage *for Joseph Cornell*," handwritten with a photograph of one of Kunitz's own collages. *Craft Horizons*, 34 (October 1974), 38.

2. "Words for the Unknown Makers," p. 35. "A Blessing of Women" was reprinted in the *New York Times*, February 14, 1975, p. 37, and in the *Iowa Review*, 5 (Spring 1974), 86-87.

3. "The Layers," *American Poetry Review*, 8 (January-February, 1979), 48. The information about the title of this poem as a section title and about his forthcoming volume of poems was supplied to me by Stanley Kunitz in a letter, January 21, 1979.

4. *Atlantic*, 243 (January 1979), 83.

Selected Bibliography

This bibliography begins with a list of Stanley Kunitz's books of poetry and prose and continues with those that he translated and those that he edited. Important articles and reviews by him follow. After these, some of his contributions to other books are listed. The arrangement is chronological, and all except the first three are annotated.

In the Secondary Sources, the pieces of consequence are those by Hagstrum and Mills. Some citations relevant in the Notes and References are omitted here.

PRIMARY SOURCES

1. Books of Poetry and Prose

Intellectual Things. New York: Doubleday, Doran, 1930.
Passport to the War. A Selection of Poems. New York: Henry Holt, 1944.
Selected Poems, 1928–1958. Boston: Atlantic-Little, Brown, 1958.
The Testing-Tree. Poems. Boston: Atlantic-Little, Brown, 1971.
The Terrible Threshold. Selected Poems, 1940–1970. London: Secker & Warburg, 1974.
A Kind of Order, A Kind of Folly: Essays and Conversations. Boston: Atlantic-Little, Brown, 1975.
The Poems of Stanley Kunitz, 1928–1978. Boston: Atlantic-Little, Brown, 1979.

2. Books Translated

Poems of Akhmatova. Selected, Translated and Introduced by Stanley Kunitz with Max Hayward. Boston: Atlantic-Little, Brown, 1973.
Story Under Full Sail by Andrei Voznesensky. Translated from the Russian by Stanley Kunitz with Vera Reck, Maureen Sager, Catherine Leach. Garden City, New York: Doubleday, 1974.
Orchard Lamps by Ivan Drach. Edited and translated by Stanley Kunitz. Sheep Meadow Press, 1978.

3. Books Edited

Living Authors: A Book of Biographies. Ed. by Dilly Tante [pseud.]. New York: H. W. Wilson, 1933.
Authors Today and Yesterday. A Companion Volume to Living Authors. With Howard Haycraft; Wilbur C. Hadden, ed. asst. New York: H. W. Wilson, 1933.

The Junior Book of Authors. With Howard Haycraft. New York: H. W. Wilson, 1934.

British Authors of the Nineteenth Century. With Howard Haycraft. New York: H. W. Wilson, 1936.

American Authors, 1600–1900. A Biographical Dictionary of American Literature. With Howard Haycraft. New York: H. W. Wilson, 1938.

Twentieth Century Authors. A Biographical Dictionary of Modern Literature. With Howard Haycraft. New York: H. W. Wilson, 1942.

British Authors Before 1800. A Biographical Dictionary. With Howard Haycraft. New York: H. W. Wilson, 1952.

Twentieth Century Authors. First Supplement. With Vineta Colby. New York: H. W. Wilson, 1955.

Poems of John Keats. New York: Crowell, 1965.

European Authors, 1000–1900. A Biographical Dictionary of European Literature. With Vineta Colby. New York: H. W. Wilson, c. 1967.

World Authors, 1950–1970. Ed. John Wakeman. Stanley Kunitz, Editorial Consultant.

4. Selected Articles and Reviews

"Dilly Tante Observes," column beginning in January 1928 in *Wilson Bulletin for Librarians* (title changed to *Wilson Library Bulletin*, September 1939). Continued as "The Roving Eye" with initials "S. J. K." Final column: *Wilson Library Bulletin*, 17 (March 1943), 562. As titles of column suggest, this monthly piece by Kunitz in the H. W. Wilson Company house organ is informal and anecdotal with interesting incidental and topical comments.

"Creative Writing Workshop," *Education*, 73 (November 1952), 152–56. Both this and the report that follows are valuable for an account by Kunitz of his teaching aims and methods.

"Seminar in the Arts," *Education*, 73 (November 1952), 172–76.

"American Poetry's Silver Age," *Harper's*, 219 (October 1959), 173–79. "An improbable dialogue" between The Poet and The Young Man, this piece is an excellent survey of the poetic scene from Eliot and Frost to Ginsberg.

"Process and Thing: A Year of Poetry," *Harper's*, 221 (September 1960), 96+. The second of Kunitz's yearly surveys; comments on about a dozen of the year's books with acute observations about poetry.

"New Books," *Harper's*, 223 (August 1961), 86–91. The third of Kunitz's yearly surveys; as above.

"Frost, Williams, and Company," *Harper's*, 225 (October 1962), 100–103+. The fourth of Kunitz's yearly surveys; as above.

"Auden on Poetry: A Conversation with Stanley Kunitz," *Atlantic*, 218 (August 1966), 94–102. Like Kunitz's conversations with Robert Lowell and Andrei Voznesensky (both included in *A Kind of Order*), here it is mostly the other poet, W. H. Auden, who is heard, but there are some valuable observations about Kunitz, too.

5. Books Contributed To

"Poetry's Silver Age: An Improbable Dialogue," in *Writing in America*, ed. by John Fischer and Robert B. Silvers. New Brunswick, N.J.: Rutgers University Press, 1960. A reprint of Kunitz's 1959 survey of the contemporary poetic scene for *Harper's*, cited above.

"The Taste of Self (On Theodore Roethke's 'In a Dark Time')," in *The Contemporary Poet as Artist and Critic*, ed. by Anthony Ostroff. Boston: Little, Brown, 1964. Kunitz's close analysis of his friend Roethke's poem for Ostroff's symposia.

"On 'Father and Son,'" in *The Contemporary Poet as Artist and Critic*, ed. by Anthony Ostroff. Boston: Little, Brown, 1964. Kunitz's comments on his own poem for Ostroff's symposia.

"Out of the Cage," in *Randall Jarrell, 1914–1965*, ed. by Robert Lowell, Peter Taylor, and Robert Penn Warren. New York: Farrar, Straus, 1967. Brief, personal, this memoir mostly comments on Jarrell's poem "The Woman at the Washington Zoo" as representative of the pain in Jarrell's poetry.

SECONDARY SOURCES

In preparing this first full-length study of Kunitz, I have consulted only materials in periodicals and books.

1. Biography

Useful biographical accounts are those in *Current Biography*, 1959, and the *Encylopaedia Judaica* (1971). Some additional biographical facts are in Michael True, *Worcester Poets. With Notes Toward a Literary History* (Worcester: The Worcester County Poetry Association, 1972), pp. 27–30. An account of Kunitz's career compiled in 1974 is in *Contemporary Authors*, volumes 41–44. *Twentieth Century Authors. First Supplement (1955)*, edited by Kunitz himself with Vineta Colby, contains no Kunitz entry, though it includes entries for his peers, Lowell, Roethke, and Wilbur. Since he was by then the Editorial Consultant, not an editor, Kunitz prepared an autobiographical sketch for *World Authors, 1950–1970* (ed. by John Wakeman), H. W. Wilson's "companion" to *Twentieth Century Authors* and its *First Supplement*. There in two pages he gives a narrative of his life; the subsequent commentary and appended bibliography make this entry the best survey of him and his work in reference volumes. Some few details here and there in my text are from correspondence I had with Kunitz while I was writing this book and from a visit with him the afternoon of August 20, 1975, at his summer home in Provincetown. Generally I have not thought it necessary to document these specifically. Some published accounts with biographical data are listed immediately below. The anonymous "Craft Interview" in the *New York Quarterly* and the Davis, Lupher, and Ryan interviews are referred to in the Notes as, respectively, *New York Quarterly, Contemporary Literature, Yale Literary Magazine,* and *Iowa Review.*

ALLEN, HENRY. "The Poets' Poet: Stanley Kunitz at the Library of Congress," *Potomac* (Washington *Post* Sunday Supplement), January 9, 1975, pp. 10+. A brief account of Kunitz's life and an interview with him; focusses on his work as Consultant in Poetry to the Library of Congress.

ANON. "Craft Interview with Stanley Kunitz," *New York Quarterly,* 1 (Fall 1970), 9–22. As the title suggests, mostly about the craft of poetry. Valuable, with some interesting biographical information, especially about Kunitz's work with the Fine Arts Work Center in Provincetown.

BRANTLEY, ROBIN. "A Touch of the Poet," *New York Times Magazine,* September 7, 1975, pp. 80–83. An excellent commentary on and description of Kunitz's gardens at his homes in New York City and in Provincetown. "Gardening," Kunitz says, "is a very deep, intimate part of my poetic life."

[DAVIS, CYNTHIA]. "An Interview with Stanley Kunitz—Conducted by Cynthia Davis," *Contemporary Literature,* 15 (Winter 1974), 1–14. An excellent, wide-ranging interview.

GROSS, HARVEY. "Stanley Kunitz, Action and Incantation," *Antaeus,* 30/31 (Spring 1978), 283–295. An interview mostly on prosody.

LOXTERMAN, ALAN, moderator. "Poetry in the Classroom: A Symposium with Marvin Bell, Donald Hall, and Stanley Kunitz," *American Poetry Review,* 6 (No. 1, 1977), 9–13. A symposium on "The Continuing Revolution in American Poetry" held at the University of Virginia in January 1976 shows Kunitz giving some new considerations as well as repeating favorite ideas.

LUPHER, DAVID. "Stanley Kunitz on Poetry: A Yale Lit Interview," *Yale Literary Magazine,* 136 (May 1968), 6–13. The earliest of the Kunitz interviews; photographs of Kunitz at home among his flowers and books.

MILLS, RALPH J., JR. "Kunitz, Stanley (Jasspon)," in *Contemporary Poets of the English Language,* ed. by Rosalie Murphy. New York: St. Martin's Press, 1970. As with the other entries in this excellent compilation, this one on Kunitz by Mills is brief but of great value.

RUSSELL, ROBERT. "The Poet in the Classroom," *College English,* 28 (May 1967), 580–86. An account of Kunitz's visit to a college classroom.

RYAN, MICHAEL. "An Interview with Stanley Kunitz," *Iowa Review* (Spring 1974), 76–85. His "best interview," in Kunitz's opinion.

2. Articles, Sections in Books, and Selected Reviews

BELOOF, ROBERT. "On Stanley Kunitz's 'Father and Son,'" in *The Con-*

temporary Poet as Artist and Critic, ed. by Anthony Ostroff. Boston: Little, Brown, 1964. Analysis of "Father and Son."

BRODSKY, JOSEPH. "Translating Akhmatova," *New York Review of Books*, August 9, 1973, pp. 9–10. The most severe of the critics about the quality of Kunitz's translation, but ultimately approving.

CIARDI, JOHN. "[A review of *Selected Poems*]," *Saturday Review of Literature*, 41 (September 27, 1958), 18. Concludes that "Kunitz is certainly the most neglected good poet of the last quarter-century."

ELLIOTT, GEORGE P. "[A review of *Selected Poems*]," *Accent*, 18 (Autumn 1958), 267–70. A detailed, perceptive review.

GROSS, HARVEY. *Sound and Form in Modern Poetry: A Study of Prosody from Thomas Hardy to Robert Lowell*. Ann Arbor: University of Michigan Press, 1968. Three pages of praise for Kunitz as a prosodist: "Kunitz' ear for quantity and monosyllabic harmonies is nearly unmatched among American poets."

HAGSTRUM, JEAN H. "The Poetry of Stanley Kunitz: An Introductory Essay," in *Poets in Progress*, ed. by Edward Hungerford. Evanston, Ill.: Northwestern University Press, 1967. The most complete and thorough of the articles on Kunitz's poetry.

HUDDLE, DAVID. "In Fierce Decay a Stripe of Honey: The Poetry of Stanley Kunitz," *Northern New England Review*, 1 (1975), 20–26. A fine commentary on Kunitz's poetry by a young poet; especially good on the differences between the early verse and that of *The Testing-Tree*.

KERMODE, FRANK. "[A review of *Selected Poems*]," *Spectator*, July 17, 1959, p. 81. A brief, perceptive review. "A Roman Thief" is "a splendid maledictory poem," and Kunitz is "indeed a big poet."

LOWELL, ROBERT. "On Stanley Kunitz's 'Father and Son,'" in *The Contemporary Poet as Artist and Critic*, ed. by Anthony Ostroff. Boston: Little, Brown, 1964. A relaxed, informal analysis of "Father and Son."

MERCIER, VIVIAN. "[A review of *Selected Poems*]," *Commonweal*, 69 (February 13, 1959), 523. "Like several of the greatest modern poets, Kunitz speaks more directly to us—and more richly, too—as he grows older."

MESIC, MICHAEL. "[A review of *Poems of Akhmatova*]," *Poetry*, 124 (July 1974), 238–40. The Akhmatova translations "are excellent, better than one ever expected them to be, conscientiously respectful of the original and aware of the demands of English."

MILES, JOSEPHINE. "On Stanley Kunitz's 'Father and Son,'" in *The Contemporary Poet as Artist and Critic*, ed. by Anthony Ostroff. Boston: Little, Brown, 1964. Another excellent analysis of "Father and Son."

MILLS, RALPH J., JR. *Contemporary American Poetry*. New York: Random House, 1966. Along with Hagstrum's essay, one of the best essays on Kunitz's poetry.

———. "Kunitz, Stanley (Jasspon)," in *Contemporary Poets of the English Language*, ed. by Rosalie Murphy. New York: St. Martin's Press, 1970.

The best brief exposition of Kunitz's ideas and biography.

Moss, STANLEY. "[A review of *The Testing-Tree*]," *Nation*, 213 (September 20, 1971), 250. A superior review of *The Testing-Tree*. "Kunitz' accomplishment . . . should occasion a national holiday."

MUCHNIC, HELEN. "[A review of *Poems of Akhmatova*]," *New York Times Book Review*, October 21, 1973, p. 6. Though the translations are "on the whole as good as any we have had so far," they "are not great poems."

NYREN, DOROTHY, comp. and ed. *A Library of Literary Criticism. Modern American Literature.* New York: Frederick Ungar, 1971. Collects comments from ten reviews, 1930–1959.

ROSENTHAL, M. L. *The Modern Poets. A Critical Introduction.* New York: Oxford University Press, 1965. Though brief, like most of Rosenthal's discussions, judicious and discriminating.

———. "[A review of *Selected Poems*]," *Nation*, 187 (October 11, 1958), 214. "Stanley Kunitz has a rich lyrical style; sometimes a redundancy of it."

RUSSELL, ROBERT. "The Poet in the Classroom," *College English*, 28 (May 1967), 580–86. In addition to a portrayal of Kunitz talking with students, this article contains some explication of "The Science of the Night," "The Way Down," and other poems.

SCHORER, MARK. "[A review of *Passport to the War*]," *New York Times*, March 26, 1944, p. 21. The "metaphysical" style characteristic of the early Kunitz "Now . . . has become entirely his own, and he writes with terse, fresh imagery at nearly every point."

VINE, RICHARD. "[A review of *A Kind of Order, A Kind of Folly*]," *Salmagundi*, No. 36 (Winter 1977), 117–123. Not given nearly the consideration that it deserved, the book almost in this review alone has its superb qualities and importance truly estimated.

WAGONER, DAVID. "[A review of *Selected Poems*]," *Poetry*, 93 (December 1958), 174–78. A detailed review with analysis of two of Kunitz's poems; comments that *Selected Poems* should "end . . . Kunitz's quiet Thirty Years War for a place among the very best poets of our time."

WINTERS, YVOR. "[A review of *Intellectual Things*]," *New Republic*, 63 (June 4, 1930), 77. "The experience in which Mr. Kunitz deals is normal, rich and complex; he is firm on his feet, and, now and again, quick on them."

WRIGHT, JAMES. "[A review of *Selected Poems*]," *Sewanee Review*, 67 (January-March 1959), 330–36. "In the hands of this poet, the subject [of love] flinches and wails. It is not pretty. It has grandeur."

ZABEL, MORTON DAUWEN. "[A review of *Intellectual Things*]," *Poetry*, 36 (July 1930), 218–23. ". . . Kunitz plunges into his elaborate imagery, conceits, and phraseology with none of the hesitation that detains the poet stricter in matters of form and logic."

Index